The 6th Connaug

BELFAST NATIONALISTS
AND THE GREAT WAR

16th (Irish) Division Cross at Guillemont

The 6th Connaught Rangers

BELFAST NATIONALISTS
AND THE GREAT WAR

6TH CONNAUGHT RANGERS
RESEARCH PROJECT
2011

Community Relations Council

This publication has received support from the Northern Ireland Community Relations Council which aims to promote a pluralist society characterised by equity, respect for diversity, and recognition of interdependence. The views expressed do not necessarily reflect those of the Council.

First published 2008, second edition (updated and enlarged) 2011 by the 6th Connaught Rangers Research Project, 426 Falls Road, Belfast, BT12 6EN production by Ulster Historical Foundation, 49 Malone Road, Belfast, BT9 6RY www.ancestryireland.com

Cover design by David Graham
Engravings used in the publication by artist Harry Clarke
and reproduced from *Ireland's Memorial Records 1914–1918*

ISBN: 978-1-903688-35-9

Printed by W & G Baird
Design and typesetting by FPM Publishing

Contents

6th Connaught Rangers Project
Steering Committee

Siobhán Deane Brennan
Sean Curry
Cathal and Bernadette Donaghy
Harry Donaghy
Prof. Richard Grayson
Brian Hanley
Jimmy McDermott
Robin and Margaret McKillen
Seán O'Hare
Jonathan Savage

A wreath in memory of the 6th Battalion was laid by some members of the Steering
Committee at the memorial on Frezenberg Ridge, October 2010.
Left of right: Cathal and Bernadette Donaghy, Siobhán Deane,
Seán O'Hare, Robin McKillen and Harry Donaghy

Acknowledgements

This publication is the result of work carried out by the 6th Connaught Rangers Research Project. It is by no means a contribution to the glorification of the senseless slaughter of the First World War.

It is not an exhaustive piece of research, rather a snap shot of young Nationalists who joined the 6th Connaught Rangers from the Falls and other areas of Belfast. We hope to continue the work of the project and would appreciate support from families, friends and any other interested parties in this complex and fascinating period of local history.

The 6th Connaught Rangers Research Project would like to extend our thanks and appreciation to all those individuals and groups and supporting organisations whose help and assistance has made the revised second edition of this book possible.

Special thanks to Sean Curry and the Committee of The An Eochair/Clondara Historical and Cultural Group, who initiated the Project, and to Ray Mullan of the Northern Ireland Community Relations Council for the contribution to the printing and production costs of this book.

To Prof. Richard Grayson of Goldsmiths, University of London, and Fintan Mullan of the Ulster Historical Foundation for their guidance and advice to the Project. To Brian Hanley, Jimmy McDermott, Jonny Savage, Siobhán Deane, Seán O'Hare, Cathal Donaghy and Robin McKillen who have contributed new and updated articles, photographs, postcards and family memorabilia, our grateful appreciation.

Thanks also to Christy Roche and Tim Carey of Fermoy, Co. Cork for their help with the photographs and for the guided tour of the Barracks in Fermoy in March 2010.

We would also like to express thanks to The Fellowship of Messines Association 'Leaders for Transformation' Project, under the I.F.I. Community Bridges Programme, the Consensus Initiative of the Belfast Unemployed Resource Centre for support and assistance given also.

Finally to all the individuals, friends and well-wishers from home and abroad, who have given their support to the work and efforts of the Project, we extend our thanks for the letters of support and words of encouragement given to us by you all.

The 6th Connaught Rangers Research Project
and Steering Committee

In Memoriam:
Our Irish Dead

*(suggested by yesterday's impressive parade and
Memorial Mass in St Peter's Pro-Cathedral)**

Oh, gallant dead who gave your lives for Ireland.
Great-hearted children of a valorous race,
With bowed and reverent heads, we pay you homage
Here at God's altar in this holy place.

The mothers' eyes shall burn with tears of sorrow,
And comrades thoughts shall travel o'er the waves
To devastated fields in France and Flanders,
Where nestle close your rough and unmarked graves.

Never in any cause did great men battle
With love and loyalty to equal yours.
The world shall read the story of your offering,
And learn in truth how Ireland's name endures.

*Source: Poem reproduced from an *Irish News* report in the post-war period

Introduction

Harry Donaghy

The Project was initiated originally by members of the An Eochair Clondara Historical & Cultural Group which is based in Belfast. The question of 'Irish Nationalists and WW1' was a subject that the Group had a keen interest in and wished to develop further. Some members of the Group had family relatives who had enlisted, along with hundreds of others from the Falls Road area, in the Connaught Rangers Regiment at the outbreak of World War One in August 1914.

Many of these men were members of the Irish National Volunteers and were ardent supporters of the Irish Parliamentary Party who, under the leadership of John Redmond and Joe Devlin, were campaigning for 'Home Rule' for Ireland.

It was agreed that in order to take the Project forward other local people should be encouraged to become involved as well. A letter from the Group outlining the aims of the Project, and with an appeal for information from other interested members of the general public, was sent to the *Irish News*, which published an article about the proposed research Project on the 26th April 2006.

The interest generated by the article resulted in a number of interested local people coming forward to take part. They assisted in forming 'The 6th Connaught Rangers Research Project' and the time and commitment given by them on a voluntary basis has proved invaluable to the whole endeavour. Through the photographs, letters, documents, medals and related memorabilia supplied by them, and others involved, the human stories of men from that time in our common and shared history could finally be told.

Through the support and backing from the Northern Ireland Community Relations Council the Project was enabled to launch a booklet on the research that had been carried out. The original publication was hosted and launched on the 19th November 2008 in the Office of the then Lord Mayor, Councillor Tom Hartley, at Clarendon Dock. The event was attended by a wide range of people from groups and organisations from across the sectarian and political divides here.

Although only 1200 copies of the original booklet were printed, the interest generated and the requests that came in from home and abroad exceeded all expectations. Literally, from Newry to New Zealand, enquiries came in from people wishing to obtain copies!

The success of and the resulting interest in the original publication led all those involved in the Project to seriously consider compiling a 'Revised Edition' with additional stories, photographs and historical material.

Contact was made again with Fintan Mullan from the Ulster Historical Foundation and the Community Relations Council was approached in regard to supporting a new edition.

We would like to take this opportunity to express our sincere thanks and appreciation to all who have helped make the new publication possible. The financial support and assistance from N.I. Community Relations Council, The Fellowship of Messines Association 'Leaders for Transformation' Project, The Consensus Initiative of the Belfast Unemployed Resource Centre and all of those who have contributed by way of articles and related historical details.

BACKGROUND

Ireland at that time had become a virtual armed camp over the question of Home Rule. The country stood on the brink of Civil War between those Irish Nationalists who were passionately for Home Rule and those Irish Unionists who were as equally passionately against it. From 1912 onwards, when the Ulster Volunteer Force was formed and led by Sir Edward Carson and Sir James Craig, the 'Home Rule Crisis' had deepened significantly. Massive amounts of arms were imported from Europe by both the 'pro' and 'anti' Home Rule camps. Tens of thousands had joined both the Ulster Volunteer Force and the Irish National Volunteers and both were drilling with the imported arms for the showdown between them that both armed camps believed was imminent.

The Falls Road, like the rest of Ireland at the time, was in a state of ferment and expectation. The inexorable drift into all-out Civil War seemed unstoppable.

Political events in the seemingly far away Balkans region of south-eastern Europe, in June of 1914, were about to set the spark to a conflagration that had been building for decades between the Great Imperial Powers. Unknowingly, for millions of citizens and subjects from across the continent, a cataclysm of unprecedented fury was about to engulf them and the nations and peoples of Europe and beyond.

The island of Ireland and its competing factions would not be immune from the impending maelstrom.

Belfast and the British Army
before 1916

Jimmy McDermott

In January 1919, on the same day that the first Dáil met in Dublin, an ambush by Irish Volunteers sparked what came to be known variously as the Anglo-Irish War, the Tan War or the War of Independence. By 1922 this struggle was settled by a Treaty which created two separate administrations in Ireland after which republicans and the forces of the new Irish Free State fought a bitter Civil War. Within the Nationalist community throughout Ireland, as a result of the 1919–22 War, attitudes hardened, and any contact with British armed forces came to be regarded as pernicious. Republicans especially tended to downplay the role that any of their antecedents had played in any branch of the British armed forces.

The consequences of this were that a misconception took hold of public consciousness that service in the British Army was largely Protestant and unionist. There are of course many reasons for this. Members of the Ulster Volunteer Force (U.V.F.) did indeed join in large numbers in 1914. This was to show their loyalty to Britain and demonstrate their opposition to Home Rule. The 36th Ulster Division suffered terrible casualties on the Western Front and Unionists continue to commemorate their sacrifices to the present day. They have every right to do so but it is only in more recent years that leading republicans too have acknowledged the huge cost that soldiers from Ireland generally paid for their service in the Great War.

In recent years Lord Mayors of Belfast, Alex Maskey and Tom Hartley, of Sinn Féin have laid wreaths at the Cenotaph in the City Hall to the dead of the First World War and have engaged in various types of commemoration. In so doing, they are recognising the *realpolitick* of the Nationalist population's relationship with the British Army before 1916. There had, in fact, always been a long tradition of service in the British Forces among the Catholic population.

Let us take Belfast as an example. Despite the sectarian hostility endemic to the city British soldiers attracted admiration from both unionist and nationalist newspapers. There are many examples of obituaries lauding certain individuals' military careers but this case may help to illustrate the contemporary view. On Saturday 18th July 1914, the *Belfast Telegraph*, which at this time supported Sir Edward Carson and the U.V.F., carried a eulogy and photograph of a Catholic ex-sergeant. Without any trace of irony the article praises John Walsh's long service including his presence at the capture of Sevastopol in 1856, during the Crimean War. It goes on to mention the old soldier's funeral from St Paul's Church on the Falls Road and sent condolences to his family. Articles which were similar were common in the *Irish News*.

Many Belfast Nationalists who were strongly in favour of Home Rule saw no problem in joining the British Army. For example in Belfast in 1914 there were 3,250 members of the Irish Volunteers. Before the outbreak of the Great War they were pledged to fight and die for Home Rule. Following John Redmond's advice to 'go as far as the firing line extends', by September 1914 over half of the 3,250 Irish Volunteers in Belfast had enlisted, with only 1,380 remaining in the Irish National Volunteers, as those now following Redmond had started calling themselves by February 1915. Another 200 formed the core of the anti-Redmond Irish Volunteers.[1]

While there were always hardline republicans who took a dim view of anyone joining the British Army, very often individuals who enlisted in the British Army in the Great War came back to give service to the Republican cause. In Cork, Tom Barry is an obvious example, but Belfast also had many such ex-servicemen in the republican ranks. One such individual was Sean Montgomery, who explains in his memoir of his time in the Irish Volunteers, 'drilling went on till the First World War started'. John Redmond made speeches in which he stated that 'the Irish Volunteers would defend Ireland from the Germans'. Joe Devlin, too, started recruiting for the formation of the 16th and 10th Irish Divisions. Many good Irishmen believed that they were going to fight for the freedom of small nations including Ireland.

After the war Sean Montgomery recalls recrimination from some Belfast republicans who had not joined the British Forces. When the Irish Volunteers regrouped 'the people were abused by those who should have known better'.[2]

Joe Devlin, flanked by Hibernians at a pro-war rally, Belfast

In fact of course the boom and slump of an industrial economy such as Belfast's had always made the prospect of an army career attractive to both Protestants and Catholics. John Christie, a Protestant from the Shankill area, who was a bugler in the pre-war U.V.F., would have been much the same age as Sean Montgomery when he joined the British Army for the Great War. His reasons for joining would have had much in common with his Catholic counterpart. John Christie worked in the Ulster Spinning Company on the Falls Road and he recalled 'I hated it. I hated it. It was an awful place to work in those days'. He didn't see military service as an act of patriotism so much as an 'escape route out ... of the mill ... for surely life holds more than the mill can offer'.[3]

The Army could indeed offer a steady wage, a pension, a uniform, travel, adventure, prestige and the prospect of promotion. In the period up to the Great War, the Irish Nationalist demand was for Home Rule not a republic. Most Nationalists changed their views dramatically in the aftermath of the Easter Rising. It was the ex-British soldier and Irish Volunteer Commander, Sir Maurice Moore, who foresaw most clearly the sea-change in Nationalist opinion about the British Army: 'a few unknown men shot in a barrack yard have embittered a whole nation'.[4] The 'Khaki' election of December 1918 showed how prophetic Maurice Moore's words were. Sinn Féin completely obliterated the Irish Parliamentary Party and emerged with a mandate, as they believed, for complete Irish independence. Partly this was a consequence of Sinn Féin's strong opposition to the threatened imposition of conscription in Ireland. Many Irishmen who had joined the British Army for honourable motives found their actions were now out of favour. The survivors of the trenches often chose to stay mute about the 1914–1918 period and only slowly now can the experiences of Irish soldiers be fairly evaluated.

REFERENCES

1   National Archive, Kew. CO904/94–96: RIC Reports July 1914–April 1915.
2   Sean Montgomery Memoir. In writer's personal possession.
3   Billy McKeen and Jack Christie. 'A Veteran Returns' *Battle Lines: Journal of the Somme Association*, 4 (1991), pp. 30–31.
4   Eamon Phoenix, *Northern Nationalism: Nationalist Politics, Partition and the Catholic Minority in Northern Ireland, 1890–1940*, Belfast, 1994, p. 18.

The Connaught Rangers:
A Brief Outline

Seán O'Hare

On the 3rd of October 1793 the following notice appeared in the *Connaught Journal*:

God save the King

> Whereas the Hon. Colonel de Burg is appointed by his majesty to raise a regiment immediately – and intends paying his respects in person to his friends in Connaught without delay – this is to give notice that houses of rendezvous will be opened in Galway, Portumna, etc., and great encouragement given to young men of good character who wish to serve our beloved Monarch under so distinguished an officer.

The notice went on to state that the Clanricarde standard would be on display for the occasion, and the regiment would be named the Connaught Rangers. This advert would lead to the deaths of thousands of young Irishmen in many foreign conflicts not of their country's making. At their formation, like so many Irish and Scottish Highland regiments, the Rangers were deemed more expendable than their English counterparts, and were sent to far flung theatres of war for long periods. The old maxim being that the further the regimental home base was from Westminster the less fuss there would be about casualties.

The Connaught Rangers were to have a long and illustrious career in the service of the British Empire. The regiment won their first battle honours in the Peninsular Campaign 1808–14, under the command of the Duke of Wellington, where they were to the fore in many of the major battles that took place there in the war with France. In 1834 the regiment was billeted on the island of Corfu where they were presented with their new regimental colours. On the new colours were the battle honours from the Peninsular Campaign, North America, the West Indies and the Mediterranean before going on to serve in the Crimean War with Russia in 1854. It was due to their tenacity in the battles of Alma, Inkerman and Sevastopol that they gained the nickname the 'Devils Own'. Many of the men who were later to join the 6th Battalion at the outbreak of the First World War came from the streets around the Falls Road, which were named in commemoration of these and other Crimean War battles.

The formation of the Connaughts back in 1793 coincided with the first stirrings of Irish republicanism, sparked by the formation of the Society of United Irishmen in

1791, leading to the 1798 rebellion, and all that was to follow down to the present day.

On Christmas day of 1798, a year in which over thirty thousand had died in the uprising in Ireland, the Connaught Rangers sailed for India. The regiment later took part in the suppression of the Indian Mutiny in 1857. Ironically it was to be in India sixty-three years later that the conflicting ideals of militant republicanism and old style nationalism would be confronted by members of the regiment.

In 1877 they were sent to South Africa where they fought in the Kaffir War, and in 1879, the Zulu War, where the 88th took part in the final defeat of Chief Cetywayo (Chattaweo) in Zululand.

At Moltan in 1881 the regiment was renamed the 1st Battalion Connaught Rangers. The 2nd Battalion Connaught Rangers came from the 94th regiment of foot which was formed up in Scotland in September 1793. In the Boer War of 1899–1901 they again fought with distinction.

At the outbreak of the First World War the 1st Battalion were sent from India to Europe with the Lahore division. The 2nd Battalion left Dublin for Aldershot to join the British Expeditionary Force (B.E.F.) The 2nd Battalion of the Connaught Rangers were virtually wiped out during the retreat from Mons where they held back the German advance while the B.E.F. regrouped. This carnage hardly merits a footnote among the countless tragedies of this most futile of wars.

With the onset of the 'the war to end all wars' four more reserve battalions of Connaught Rangers were raised. It was in the 6th reserve battalion that so many Belfast Nationalists enlisted, many of whom were members of the Irish National Volunteers. This is where the story of our grandfathers begins. For the lucky ones their hell was to last another four years.

Connaught Rangers spent about 60% of their time as fatigue parties, repairing trenches and carrying up ammunition and rations. This is a typical rest station for a fatigue party

At the outbreak of the War the majority of the men serving in the regiment would of course have come from the province of Connacht, though in the final years of the regiment's existence many of those who enlisted would be Nationalists from West Belfast.

On the Falls Road, indeed all over Ireland, they rallied to the call of their political leaders, John Redmond and Joe Devlin of the Irish Parliamentary Party. Their eagerness was fuelled as much by poverty as politics. Their hope was for 'the freedom of small nations' and a promised reward of Home Rule for Ireland.

On Easter Monday 1916, while the 6th Connaughts were being bled to death around what was left of the towns of Hulluch and Mazingarbe in Belgium, in Dublin a group of men in green uniforms assembled with arms, and declared the Irish Republic. The men of the Connaughts, like the majority of Irish people at the time, would have deemed the rising as futile. They believed that by their service in the War they would achieve far more for Ireland. All this was to change. Brutal measures against the insurgents by the British government would lead to a resurgence of militant republicanism and the death knell of Redmondism as the leading force of Irish Nationalism.

Near the village of Wytschaete in Belgium, where so many Rangers died, a celtic cross was erected by local people to the memory of the Irish soldiers who gave their lives there. A similar cross was erected in the village of Guillemont to Irish soldiers who died in its defence. The inscription reads, in Latin and Gaelic, 'To the Glory of God and the Honour of Ireland'.

As for the men who returned, there were no flag waving throngs to welcome them home to the new situation in Ireland. Their Home Rule politics had lost the argument to the republican cause.

Many survivors went home to a quiet life with their families. Many would later join the new army of the Irish Free State. A large number of ex-Rangers would also join the I.R.A. where their training and expertise were put to good use in the struggle for independence and in the defence of the Catholic ghettos of Belfast in the early 1920s. Tom Barry arguably the best military leader in the War of Independence had been a sergeant in the Connaught Rangers.

Whatever path each chose on returning home, we should remember them all with equal respect. I leave the last words to a songwriter, Father O'Neill of St Peter's parish, Falls Road, where many of those who enlisted in 1914 with the 6th Connaughts were born:

> T'was Britannia bade our wild geese fled that small nations might be free
> But their lonely graves are by Suvlas waves or the shores of the great North Sea.

The Foggy Dew

On the 12th June 1922 at Windsor Castle the regiment was thanked by King George V for their services to the Empire, he accepted their colours for safe-keeping and disbanded the Connaught Rangers.

The 6th Connaught Rangers at War

Richard S. Grayson

THE POLITICS OF RECRUITMENT

The outbreak of war posed Nationalist leaders with a dilemma. The traditional dictum that 'England's danger is Ireland's opportunity' meant that Nationalists might have sought to undermine the British war effort. In fact, they did exactly the reverse. On 6 August 1914, two days after Britain entered the war, the *Irish News* reported the departure on the previous day of 600 British army reservists from the Irish Volunteers who were honouring their commitment to fight, and the Nationalist leadership soon went beyond simply ensuring that reservists did as they were obliged.

There were several reasons for Nationalists to volunteer. The army offered a way out of unemployment and poverty. The prospect of defending plucky little Catholic Belgium against German aggression was a stirring cause. Meanwhile, more than that, the political leadership of Nationalism saw an opportunity for Ireland to show that it could be trusted with Home Rule if it was willing to fight for the British Empire in its hour of need. That led initially to John Redmond's offer of the Irish Volunteers for the defence of Ireland, so that British troops could leave Ireland for the front. A reward for this attitude was the passage of Home Rule as law on 18 September, though its implementation was suspended for the duration of the war, and there would be special (though as yet undefined) provision for Ulster. Nationalists celebrated, although as the war dragged on, they would find it ever harder to use the promise of Home Rule at some point in the future to restrain more radical elements in their ranks.

However, both Volunteer groups were soon to join up. The 36th (Ulster) Division was formed for the Ulster Volunteer Force, and by mid-September Redmond was trying to arrange for a similar 'Irish Brigade' to be set up as an umbrella for the Irish Volunteers to join up. His speech at Woodenbridge, County Wicklow, on 20 September called on Irishmen to enlist. This led to a split in the Irish Volunteers. Across the whole island, approximately 93% of the Volunteers backed Redmond, although Eoin MacNeill controlled much of the official machinery and so Redmond's majority split to form the Irish National Volunteers.[1]

Following the split, Redmond turned to ensuring that enough Volunteers joined the British army to make real the idea of an Irish Brigade, and he was successful in persuading Kitchener that the 16th (Irish) Division, specifically 47 Brigade within it, should form such a unit.[2] With a division containing three brigades and support troops, and each brigade containing four battalions of up to 1,000 men, there was space

Joe Devlin wearing a sash of the exclusively Catholic Ancient Order Of Hibernians, a fraternal
society founded in the United States where it claimed 100,000 members. He was a member
the A.O.H. and locally they were in effect Devlin's political machine

for as many as 4,000 in 47 Brigade. At a mass meeting in Belfast's Clonard Picture
House on 25 October, Redmond turned up the heat on those considering joining up.
How humiliated Irishmen would feel, Redmond said, 'if when this war was over, they
had to admit that their rights and liberties had been saved by the sacrifices of other
men, while the Irishmen remained safe at home and took no risks.'[3]

A week and a half into November, Redmond's pressure was making an impact on the
numbers of I.N.V. men enrolling. On 12 November, even the *Belfast Evening Telegraph*
(usually as grudging about Nationalist recruitment efforts as the *Irish News* was about
Unionist ones) admitted that 'during the week efforts have been made by some local
Nationalists to get their men to join the army.' By that day, 300 had indicated their
willingness to join up, and the first batch of sixty mustered at Berry Street's National
Club, and then enlisted at Clifton Street. Among them were the Brennan brothers,
Robert and Michael. Both staunch Nationalists, Michael would say in later years that
he had joined up to fight for the freedom of small nations such as Belgium.[4] A steady
flow continued from the I.N.V. to Clifton Street (which was replaced in February 1915
as the Irish Brigade's recruiting office by 47 Mill Street).

As Nationalist recruits left Belfast, there were enthusiastic street scenes on 19
November when most (600) of the I.N.V. recruits departed for Fermoy. They were all
initially attached to the 6th battalion of the Connaught Rangers, though many later
went into the 7th Leinster Regiment, both battalions being part of 47 Brigade.

Thousands watched as they marched behind 'pipers in Gaelic costume, flourishing banners emblazoned with the Red Hand of the O'Neill and distinctively Irish National devices and mottoes', singing traditional Irish military songs. As they reached the Great Northern Station, further Irish songs were sung, plus 'God Save the King' and the Belfast Celtic Football Club 'war song'. Joseph Devlin arrived at the station with them and bade farewell to each recruit individually on the train, which then set off for Dublin. There was no parade in Dublin, merely tea and cigarettes, but having taken another train to Fermoy, the men were greeted there by local bands who marched with them to the Volunteer Drill Hall. There they were met by, and paraded with, I.N.V.s from the surrounding area, who accompanied them to their camp.[5] They would be there training for nearly a year when they departed to Aldershot in September 1915 for further training. This would prepare them for the five major battles in which they would take part: the Somme, Messines (Mesen), Passchendaele (Passendale), Cambrai, and the German Spring Offensive.

THE SOMME: GUILLEMONT AND GINCHY[6]

It was not until the autumn of 1915, when the war had been raging for well over a year, that Ireland's 'political' volunteer battalions began to arrive on the Western Front, first the 36th (Ulster) Division in October. The 6th Connaughts arrived at Le Havre early on 18 December 1915, with thirty-six officers and 952 other ranks. There is a common perception that men joined up in 1914, were sent to a trench, and stayed there for four years if they were lucky enough to survive. In fact, men were rarely on the frontline for more than a week, and from this time until September 1916, the battalion was periodically rotating in and out of the trenches. While at the front, often around Béthune, they were engaged in a simple routine: repair trenches, survive German bombardment, and repair trenches again. Their first fatality came on 27 January 1915, after an artillery bombardment, while they faced an enemy advance for the first time. The 6th Connaughts' machine guns held the Germans off, but lost one man: Private John Lavery, born in Warrenpoint, County Down, but living and having enlisted in Belfast.[7]

As the weather improved in the spring, the 6th Connaughts would have received news of the Easter Rising in Dublin, although there is no sign that Nationalists became Republicans overnight in the wake of either the rising or the British reaction to it. One member of the 6th Connaughts was very close at hand to the events. Michael Brennan, a staunch Nationalist, had joined the 6th Connaught Rangers after Redmond had called on Nationalists to enlist. Having been gassed and frostbitten in France, he was lying in a Dublin hospital bed when the I.R.A. took over the hospital, remaining in bed the whole time.[8]

Brennan was one of many Nationalists who had taken the view that they could advance their cause by fighting for the British rather than against them. They would have a chance to take their fight to the Germans on the Somme in September 1916. Planning for an offensive in the Somme area began at the end of 1915 as a way of making a decisive impact on overall German numbers. However, the aim of the offensive changed from February 1916 when the Germans launched their onslaught against the French at Verdun. From then on, the aim of the Somme Offensive, in which French troops would play only a relatively minor role, was to launch a diversionary attack that would ease pressure on the French who were being bled dry by wave on wave of German attack at Verdun. The British army launched its attack on 1 July 1916, with the Ulster Division engaged in some of the heaviest fighting. On just that one day, across the Division, there were approximately 5,550 casualties (with as many as 2,000 dead) and 58,000 in the British army as a whole, around one-third of them dead.

For the 6th Connaughts, while the Somme battle was being prepared and initiated,

there had been action mainly in the Loos sector. This period saw an effective raid on German lines on the night of 26/27 June in collaboration with the 7th Leinsters, and also witnessed acts of individual bravery. One was carried out by Private Patrick McKillen, an enlistee in the 6th Connaughts from the I.N.V. and a resident of Oranmore Street. On 27 July, McKillen 'continued to work his machine gun, single handed, under a heavy fire, after all the remainder of the section had been put out of action. Private McKillen stuck to his gun and held the position for 24 hours.'9

In September, 47 Brigade moved to the Somme area, close to the small village of Guillemont. On arriving in the area, the Connaughts faced the familiar routine of improving badly damaged trenches, and the Germans continued to inflict heavy casualties through shelling. On 2 September alone, the 6th Connaughts' B Company lost ten men killed, with a further thirty wounded.[10] The next day, they did what they had come to the Somme to do.

At 5am on 3 September, the battalion drew up for the attack. The whole of 47 Brigade was temporarily attached to the 20th Division. The plan was for three successive waves of troops to take the village. C and D companies of the 6th Connaughts were to attack in the first wave. In the second and third waves, platoons of B Company would plug the gaps in C Company's lines, and platoons from A Company

Christmas card sent by a 6th Bn, Connaught Ranger, Christmas 1917

would do the same for D. At 8am, the Germans received the familiar warning of an imminent attack: a heavy bombardment from British lines. Yet some of the heavy trench mortars being used in the attack fell short with tragic results. Waiting in 'Rim Trench' the Connaughts' C Company endured not only retaliatory fire from the Germans but 'friendly fire' from the British lines. By 12 noon, as the bombardment continued, casualties numbered nearly two hundred.

With C Company in no fit state for the first attack troops intended for the second wave replaced them. Then, for three minutes, the Royal Field Artillery let go 'an intense barrage' of the German front. Unlike the bombardment in late June, this was successful. Advancing on the enemy, the Connaughts found opposition weak in some places, but on the right, there was heavier resistance, but 47 Brigade soon overcame that, before cleaning up pockets of resistance holed out in various areas.

Private Thomas Hughes of the 6th Connaughts (and a native of County Monaghan) was wounded in the initial attack, but had wounds dressed and returned to the firing line. Having done so, he spotted a German machine gun which was causing great damage. Hughes ran out ahead of his company, shot the gunner and captured the gun. He was wounded doing this but went on to bring back four prisoners. For these acts of 'most conspicuous bravery and determination' Hughes was awarded the battalion's only Victoria Cross of the war.[11]

As a result of such bravery, the first three objectives had been reached before 1pm, and around 140 men of the 6th Connaughts joined an attack by other parts of the 16th Division on the final objective, the 'Sunken Road'. Meanwhile, the remainder of the battalion dug in with the 7th Leinsters to hold the territory gained until they were relieved the next day.

Among the dead officers was the 6th Connaughts' commanding officer, Lieutenant-Colonel J.S.M. Lenox-Conyngham. He was replaced on 6 September by Major Rowland Charles Feilding, an English convert to Catholicism, whose letters home to his wife provide an invaluable insight into details of the Connaughts. When Feilding took over, the 6th Connaughts had taken part in one of the few gains of the Somme campaign in the late summer months of 1916. But they had sustained heavy losses as had 47 Brigade as a whole. Of the 2,400 soldiers from the Brigade who took part, nearly half were injured in some way.[12] When Feilding joined the battalion as its CO he found 365 other ranks bivouacking at Carnoy 'amid a plague of flies'.

Of these, on 7 September, nearly 250 men and officers of the 6th Connaughts, and nearly 300 of the 7th Leinsters marched from Carnoy, where 47 Brigade had been resting briefly, towards the front. Before departing, the 6th Connaughts (and probably other Catholic soldiers in 47 Brigade), 'kneeling down in the ranks, all received General Absolution' from the division's Senior Chaplain.[13] They now had a fresh objective: German trenches close to the village of Ginchy, as part of a wider attack on the village itself, with the rest of the 16th Division. There had already been one failed British attack on Ginchy on 6 September and it was clear that the Germans were well dug-in.

At 4.45pm on 9 September, there was an intensive bombardment of the German lines for two minutes. Yet again, just like at Guillemont, some shells fell short. Fortunately, many were duds, and casualties were lighter than on 3 September. However, with duds also falling on German lines, the impact of the bombardment was not nearly as great as planned. When British troops moved forward at 4.47pm, they found the Germans 'very little disturbed'. So in the first wave of the attack, the 6th Royal Irish Regiment and the 8th Munster Fusiliers were 'mown down by a devastating fire from machine guns'. The original plan had been for the 6th Connaughts plus one company of the 7th Leinsters and two from the 11th Hampshires, to follow behind the first attack, but with the Munsters so badly hit, their men had stopped advancing. A and B companies of the Connaughts realised what had happened and stayed in their trenches, but C and D companies plus the Leinsters and Hampshires did not. When there was a pause in the fighting, they judged that it was their turn to attack. They advanced, but had moved only a few yards before they came under heavy fire. Both officers were hit and the men could make no impact on the German lines. At 5.43pm a runner was sent back with a message for Divisional H.Q. saying, 'It appears that the trench opposite is full of Germans & that they were well prepared.'

Elsewhere, 48 Brigade was more successful. By 7.30pm they had taken control of the village. But the attack on Ginchy was disastrous for the Connaughts. The simple fact was that the bombardment had done too little damage to the German lines. The War Diary noted that those who saw the German trenches 'report that it had escaped our preliminary bombardment almost entirely and that it was thickly manned'. Feilding later revealed that this trench had been overlooked in the British bombardment. It was 'hidden and believed innocuous', and was expected to be the easy part of the attack. For that reason it 'had been allocated to the tired and battered 47th Brigade.' Instead, it was 'a veritable hornets' nest'.[14]

By the evening of 9 September, the Connaughts had lost ten men during the day, with more than seventy others wounded. The battalion was withdrawn from the front the day after the attack, and spent the next ten days in billets before being moved by train north to the Bailleul area. For the 16th Division as a whole, their operations on the Somme had not been as futile as those of British soldiers in July. However, across the division, between 1 and 10 September, there were 4,090 killed, wounded or missing from 10,410 other ranks, and 240 from 435 officers. Of the 4,090 other ranks, 586 were confirmed killed and 846 were missing at the end of the month.[15] At least 1,079 of those were later confirmed killed.[16] It is appropriate that a divisional memorial now stands in Guillemont.

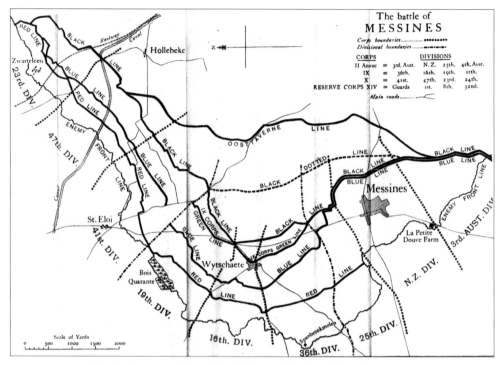

Map showing areas of attack by divisions at Messines. Advancing troops
captured the red line first, followed by the blue, green and black lines

MESSINES (MESEN)

In the aftermath of the battle of the Somme, the prospect of defeating Germany with a
decisive 'big push' seemed remote. Throughout the winter months most fighting ceased
because the weather was so bad, with heavy snow and severe frosts. From the start of
October to the end of January 1917, there were only twenty-three fatalities in the 6th
Connaughts (fifteen of those in January). But after that bitter winter, thoughts turned to
a new advance. Fighting resumed in February, with the 6th Connaughts involved in
raids, but it was not until April that the battalion was focused on a new advance.

The action at Messines (Mesen) was a prelude to the Third Battles of Ypres (Ieper),
which was planned for late July. Possession of the Messines (Mesen) ridge gave the
Germans a vantage point over the Ypres (Ieper) area, making unobserved troop
movements difficult. Holding the ridge would theoretically give the allies such an
advantage in a future attack. The preparation for Messines (Mesen) was markedly
different to that for the Somme. The officers of 47 Brigade saw a model of the area at
the end of April, and other ranks had even begun practice attacks late that month. From
mid-May, 47 Brigade used observation posts on Kemmel Hill to gain a clear view of
their target. There were also trips to the front line so that the battalion could familiarise
itself with the precise nature of the trenches to be used both for assembling and

'jumping-off'. On the last day of May the entire battalion carried out a mock attack along the lines of the planned offensive. Such preparations are a clear sign of how quickly lessons from the Somme had been learned.

By the time battalions moved to the front for the attack in early June 1917, preparations were under way to ensure that the lessons of the Somme were learned. At 3.10am on the morning of 7 June, the massive Spanbroekmolen mine was exploded under German positions, and men of the Ulster Division attacked. The contrast with 1 July 1916 was marked. The men advanced behind a creeping artillery barrage (supported by carefully targeted machine gun fire) which moved forwards with the men, a tactic which had been perfected towards the end of the battle of the Somme. Each move forward in the barrage was of about one hundred yards. So the Germans did not have the warning period immediately after a barrage had stopped in which to regroup to defend against an attack. Indeed, the men were perilously close behind the barrage – just forty yards in some cases – but they were not hit by friendly fire as the calculations were spot on.[17]

The 16th Division lined up, to the left of the Ulster Division, with 47 Brigade on the right and 49 Brigade on the left, with 48 Brigade in reserve. In 47 Brigade, the first wave was provided by the 6th Royal Irish Regiment on the right and the 7th Leinsters on the left. The 6th Connaughts were designated as 'moppers up' to go in behind their comrades from 47 Brigade, the 1st Royal Munster Fusiliers. Their target, as for the rest of the 16th (Irish) Division, was the capture of Wytschaete (Wijtschate) village. The first position was taken in little over half an hour, and the second largely by 5am, although the 7th Leinsters faced some stubborn machine gun fire. Just before reaching Wytschaete (Wijtschate) village, the Connaughts encountered a German 'strong point' which they 'rapidly overcame', capturing ninety-eight prisoners in the village itself.[18] The 6th Connaughts lost just five men, with a further thirty-two wounded and two missing. There were clear advantages to mopping up, although even the 1st Royal Munster Fusiliers out in front of the Connaughts had also lost only five men that day.

PASSCHENDAELE (PASSENDALE) AND CAMBRAI

Following Messines, the 6th Connaughts were soon in action again at the Third Battle of Ypres, at Passchendaele (Passendale). Heavy rain stopped their advance on the first day of the battle, and they dug in for the first half of August, under almost continuous fire. Twenty-four men were lost in the 6th Connaughts between 2 and 11 August. Among them was Lance-Corporal Patrick McKillen of Oranmore Street in the Falls, who had in 1916 received the divisional certificate for gallantry.[19]

Another attack was set for 16 August, and became known as the battle of Langemarck (Langemark). This attack would see the Ulster Division again in the middle (as at Messines (Mesen)) side-by-side with the 16th on their right. On the left of the 36th was the 48th Division. Within this battle order, 47 Brigade was a relief battalion. Both 48 and 49 Brigades had led for the 16th Division from 4.45am on 16 August. They incurred heavy losses though some ground had been temporarily gained. When 47

Brigade moved forward to relieve others of their division on the evening of 16 August any question of further advance was over, so the 6th Connaughts acted as stretcher-bearers. On the evening of 17 August, when the Brigade was relieved, they left third Ypres (Ieper) for good. In that first half of August, total casualties for the 6th Connaughts amounted to 249, of whom twenty-five were dead.

For the remainder of 1917, the 6th Connaughts' trenches whenever they were at the front were in a terrible condition.[20] When not in the trenches, they were training for a British attack at Cambrai, and by mid-November they were rehearsing on a replica of the German trenches. The aim at Cambrai was to break the Hindenburg Line, a formidable line of German defences built largely by Russian forced labour. It included a forward zone of around one kilometre in depth, which was relatively lightly manned in trenches. The aim of this zone was to slow down any British attack through skirmishing. That forward zone protected the main defensive lines consisting of wire up to one hundred yards in depth, concrete bunkers, deep trenches, and strong points for machine gunners.

The 16th Division was involved at Cambrai from the first, but away from the main front launching a subsidiary attack at Croiselles Heights. Its aim was to seize control of a 2,000 yard section of Tunnel Trench and Tunnel Support. The former, the target of the 6th Connaughts (the 7th Leinsters being in reserve), was about thirty feet underground, with ferro-concrete pill boxes at the top. The British had designated these Jove, Mars, Vulcan, Juno and Pluto. The first four were the targets of 16th Division.

At 6.20am on 20 November, a four minute barrage of the line began. One minute later, B Company of the 6th Connaughts leapt out of the British front line to make the 223 yard journey to Tunnel Trench. After bitter fighting the Connaughts secured their portion of Tunnel Trench, and then attacked Jove and Mars, gaining both 'after slight resistance'. German counter-attacks ensued and in one, Private Kieran White moved close to the area from which the Germans were throwing bombs, caught some of the bombs in mid-air, and threw them back before they had exploded. For this, he was awarded the Distinguished Conduct Medal. With munitions running out after an hour in Tunnel Trench, the Connaughts were forced to withdraw from Jove and consolidate at Mars. But by 8.30am supplies of bombs were starting to arrive at the front, and the Connaughts consolidated their position before being relieved by the 7th Leinsters on the evening of 22 November, having lost thirty-four killed and 109 wounded.

Following Cambrai, there was a major reorganisation of the 16th Division. At the end of January 1918, five battalions were wound up. This allowed the division to be reconfigured, like the rest of the army, into brigades of three battalions each. The 6th Connaughts remained in 47 Brigade, now joined by the 2nd Leinsters and 1st Munsters.

THE GERMAN SPRING OFFENSIVE

In the Spring of 1918, the Germans nearly won the war. From late 1917 they had strengthened their forces on the Western Front as Tsarist Russia collapsed and the war in the east ended. On 21 March, they launched what is now known as the 'Spring Offensive', gaining forty miles of allied ground in their first thrust. Eventually, they came within fifty miles of Paris, putting the city within range of their artillery. Over three hundred shells were landed on the French capital.

The 6th Connaughts were among the first caught in the advance, alongside the 2nd Leinsters which contained some remnants of the 7th. At 4.30am on 21 March, a heavy German bombardment of 47 Brigade's positions began. The bombardment made communications between brigades and battalions exceptionally difficult.[21] In the chaos, the 6th Connaughts advanced at 3.45pm at Ronssoy according to orders, without knowing that the order had actually been cancelled.

The Connaughts dug in overnight, but faced a heavy barrage again the next morning, 22 March. By this time it was becoming very difficult for Feilding to keep track of events elsewhere at the front with runners coming under heavy fire. When information did eventually reach battalion HQ it was often hours old. The Connaughts desperately tried to hold a line near to the road between Villers Faucon and Ste. Emilie, alongside battalions as diverse as the 1st Munsters, the 11th Hampshire Pioneers, the 13th Royal Sussex and 1st Hertfordshires.

For the Connaughts, steady retreat and hard fighting continued. Officer casualties had been heavy and by 5pm on 22 March Feilding was left in a command of a makeshift battalion comprised of 6th Connaughts, 1st Munsters, and 2nd Leinsters. Two men were lost through friendly fire on 23 March – an enemy aeroplane dropped a flare on the retreating soldiers which the British artillery mistook for one of its own markers and fired shrapnel on the target.

In the early hours of 27 March, word came that French reinforcements were about to pass through British lines to counter-attack the Germans. They did not, however arrive, and at daylight on 27 March, a large German force was spotted having broken through a gap between the Connaughts' position and the River Somme. By this time, enough men had regrouped for men to start to reorganise into their original battalions, and the 6th Connaughts fell back. They set up a new position from which machine gunners had a clear sight of the Germans. From this position, the Germans were held up for several hours, until fresh British troops began to force the Germans back. Here ended the Connaughts' involvement in the Spring Offensive, and the 2nd Leinsters were also back in billets by 30 March. Casualties had been heavy in the retreat. Ninety of the 6th Connaughts were killed, with over five hundred more wounded.

THE END OF THE 6TH CONNAUGHTS

When the battalion assembled at Aubigny on 31 March, just five other officers and 150 other ranks remained. As the army reorganised itself in the wake of the retreat, such a small battalion was an obvious one to be disbanded. That effectively happened on 13 April, when most of the officers and 281 men – numbers swelled by the return of the wounded – joined the 2nd Leinster Regiment, meeting former 47 Brigade comrades once in the 7th Leinsters, although that battalion was soon (on 23 April) transferred to

88 Brigade in 29th Division. A small body of headquarters officers and transport staff remained in the 6th Connaughts to form a Training Staff which was soon attached to America troops at Doudeauville. The small band of men remaining in the 6th Connaught Rangers Training Staff had much expertise to pass on to their new comrades, yet the Americans were all at the front from early July and the training staff became redundant. On 31 July 1918, the 6th Connaughts received the order that they were formally disbanded. In the entire war, at least 480 men of all ranks had lost their lives in the battalion.

REFERENCES
1   Charles Hannon, 'The Irish Volunteers and the Concepts of Military Service and defence
     1913–1924', (University College Dublin, unpublished PhD thesis, 1989), p. 105.
2   Terence Denman, *Ireland's Unknown Soldiers: The 16th (Irish) Division in the Great War*
     (1992), p. 38.
3   *Irish News*, 26 October 1914, p. 5.
4   Email to author from Michael Brennan's granddaughter, Siobhán Deane, 16 Sep. 2007.
5   *Irish News*, 20 November 1914, p. 5.
6   Unless otherwise stated, quotations regarding the 6th Connaughts in action are from:
     National Archive, Kew, WO 95/1970, 6th Connaught Rangers War Diary.
7   *Soldiers Died in the Great War.*
8   Email to author from Michael Brennan's granddaughter, Siobhán Deane, 16 Sep. 2007.
9   *Irish News*, 19 Aug. 1916, p. 5.
10   *Soldiers Died in the Great War.* Names of 2nd September casualties were not recorded until
     the next day and in the records that survive, they are mixed up with the heavy losses of
     3rd September.
11   *London Gazette*, 26 Oct. 1916.
12   National Archive, Kew, WO 95/1969, 47 Brigade War Diary.
13   Rowland Feilding, *War Letters to a Wife: France and Flanders, 1915–1919* (1929, 2001
     edn.), pp. 69 and 70.
14   Feilding, p. 72.
15   WO 95/1955.
16   This figure was reached using *Soldiers Died in the Great War.* It includes all twelve
     infantry battalions in the division, plus divisional engineers, but information on RAMC
     and RFA units is rarely present.
17   National Archive, Kew, WO 95/2491, 36th Division General Staff War Diary.
18   National Archive, Kew, WO 158/416, 16th Division 7–9 June 1917.
19   *Belfast News Letter*, 16 Aug. 1916, p. 6; 22 Aug. 1917, p. 6; 25 Aug. 1917, p. 8;
     Belfast Evening Telegraph, 21 Aug. 1916, p. 4; 26 Aug. 1916, p. 3; 27 Aug. 1917, p. 4.
20   Feilding, p. 124.
21   The 6th Connaughts and 47 Brigade war diaries for this time were lost or never made, but
     there are details of 47 Brigade's movements in the 2nd Leinsters' diary, and Feilding
     made a detailed note: National Archive, Kew, WO 95/1956, 16th Division General
     Staff War Diary.

Demoralisation
on the Home Front

Jimmy McDermott

'ENLISTMENT'

In May 1915 the First World War was not yet a year old. Charles Brett was a young Protestant officer in the overwhelmingly Catholic Connaught Rangers Regiment which was then stationed in County Cork. That same month he had seen at first hand the civilian victims of the *SS Lusitania* whose bodies were washed up on the beaches around Kinsale town, the ship having been sunk by a German torpedo. It affected Brett profoundly giving him, 'a bitter dislike of all Germans and a desire to kill as many as possible'.

His views were somewhat echoed by the Kinsale Corporation who apologised to the 'Huns for calling them Germans'. However not all Irishmen were taking the view that the sinking of the *Lusitania* was a consequence of German treachery. An anti-recruiting pamphlet, the *Spark*, pointed out that the *Lusitania* had ignored German warnings, was an auxiliary ship in the Royal Navy, was given no Royal Navy protection and was carrying munitions. The euphoric support for the war in Nationalist Ireland, so obvious in the autumn of 1914, was now being more openly challenged. Anti-recruiting propaganda was to increase even more in the next year as the names of the 900 casualties of the 10th Irish Division at Gallipoli were released. In Ireland as elsewhere, in the then unified British Isles, there was a tailing off in Volunteers but in Ireland this was often accompanied by vehemence against the British Government, the British Army and John Redmond's Irish Parliamentary Party (I.P.P.).

It has often been noted that for the Ulster Unionist family, service in the Great War is a proud part of their identity, but often markedly less so for Irish Nationalists. The recently published letters of Wilfred and Lillian Spender supply abundant evidence that the 36th Ulster Division, as well as being British patriots also saw themselves as essentially political Volunteers dedicated to either stopping Home Rule or excluding Ulster from it. The adherence of the Ulster Unionists to this viewpoint and their acceptance of the Government of Ireland Act in 1920 gave the sacrifices of the Ulstermen in the Great War a certain legitimacy. Far less so, however, for the Nationalist Volunteers who joined the Connaught Rangers with the express desire to obtain Home Rule for a 32-county Ireland within the Empire.

Charles Brett, an intelligent man, was impressed by the young volunteers of the Connaught Rangers. He thought them brave, resilient soldiers who could be 'led but not driven'. In capturing the essential individualism of the Connaught Ranger, Charlie

Brett also captured the 'particularism' of the Irish Volunteer. Like the Ulster Volunteer they had, no doubt, many personal reasons for joining the British Army but of primary concern to the Nationalist soldier was the achievement of Home Rule. For the Ulster Nationalist the exclusion of North-East Ulster from a Home Rule settlement could only result in a total sense of betrayal.

In September 1914, Prime Minister Asquith had put a Home Rule Bill on the statute book but it was not to be made law until after the Great War and there were unspecified references to special treatment for Ulster. At the outset of hostilities the Unionist leader Sir Edward Carson had been swift to volunteer the Ulster Volunteer Force as he said 'England's difficulty is not Ulster's opportunity'. John Redmond, Joe Devlin, John Dillon and the other leaders of the I.P.P. were quick to respond in kind and at Woodenbridge in September 1914 John Redmond urged National Volunteers to abandon the idea of being a Home Guard and join the British Army, 'as far as the firing line extends'. Members of Parliament for the I.P.P. such as Stephen Gwynn and John Redmond's brother Willie gave the lead by enlisting themselves.

Using the machinery of the United Irish League, the Ancient Order of Hibernians and the Irish Volunteers, the I.P.P. leaders proved adept recruiting sergeants for the British Army but their strategy involved great risks too. Not only had they made implacable enemies when a minority of Irish Volunteers split away refusing to join the British forces, but their calculations had to be for a reasonably short war with limited casualties. The I.P.P. leadership were not to know that the Great War would go through 4 stages identified by Ben Novick as

> An early rush of enthusiasm by volunteers and civilians
> A gradual decline in recruitment
> Casualties and frustration
> War weariness

The problems of the I.P.P. were further compounded by the apparent favour shown to Ulster Volunteers over Irish Volunteers. The 36th Ulster Division was seen in some Nationalist circles as more favoured than the 16th Irish Division. On top of this the 10th Irish Division was almost wiped out at Gallipoli in 1915. While John Redmond would claim that 'Ireland had a National Army in the field for the first time' writers like Katherine Tyrone represented the view of upper and middle class Dubliners that the 10th Division's sacrifices had not been recognised.

At Westminster a wartime coalition of Liberals and Conservatives ensured that the I.P.P. could no longer exert significant

---

Oglaigh na hEireann

ENROL UNDER THE GREEN FLAG

Safeguard your rights and liberties [the few left you].

Secure more.

Help your Country to a place among the nations.

Give her a national Army to keep her there.

Get a gun and do your part.

JOIN THE

IRISH VOLUNTEERS
(President: EOIN MAC NEILL)

Anti-recruitment poster by Eoin MacNeill's Irish Volunteers

leverage on the Liberal Party. Redmond himself refused to join the War Cabinet or nominate anyone from the I.P.P. to do so until Ireland obtained Home Rule. Ulster Unionists had no such inhibitions and when Sir Edward Carson joined the War Cabinet in 1915 Irish Nationalist recruitment dipped from 6,000 in April/May to 2,000 in September 1915. Although Sir Roger Casement had failed to raise an Irish Brigade to fight for a Republic in German Prisoner of War camps, and although returning Irish soldiers were received back enthusiastically by the summer of 1915, an anti-recruitment propaganda campaign was gathering strength.

PROPAGANDA

Dublin veterans of anti-recruitment since the time of the Boer War such as Arthur Griffith and Maud Gonne were again active. In Belfast Bulmer Hobson and Herbert Moore Pim produced anti-recruitment material. James Connolly and James Larkin emphasised International Workers opposition to what they saw as an Imperialist War. Connolly especially saw an element of 'economic conscription' in Dublin and wrote a pamphlet *Slums and the Trenches* in February 1916. Anti-recruitment propaganda was careful not to attack serving Irish soldiers themselves. Therefore, they would feel quite free to rejoice in the 'Battle of Ireland' but not in the 'Battle of the Somme'. Redmond

A contemporary cartoon shows just how deep the anti-Redmond sentiments were at the time

and Devlin were often advised to go to the front themselves if they were so keen and it was darkly hinted that recruitment to the British Army would be much greater if Home Rule were granted under the leadership of John Redmond. Patrick Pearse simply referred to the Great War as 'England's War'.

Up until the summer of 1916 Irish Nationalist Volunteers could take some comfort from the very able British and I.P.P. propaganda campaign. Two million recruiting posters of high quality were put up in Ireland so it was impossible to miss them. The press generally was laudatory about the bravery and sacrifices of Irish soldiers and the I.P.P. paper *Freeman's Journal* made much of Volunteers such as Tom Kettle, Maurice Moore and Willie Redmond. Despite this, Novick, for example, would argue that the losses at Sulva Bay were so influential on Irish Nationalist public opinion that the Easter Rising of 1916 was not so much transformative as the fulcrum upon which Nationalist opinion changed. There is no doubt that the Easter Rising of 1916 does mark a sea change in Irish public opinion, yet the reactions of Irish Volunteers in the British Army are harder to gauge. Richard Grayson has pointed out that there was greater suspicion of Irish private soldiers after the Rising but Jane Leonard has stated that most Irish officers in the British Army regarded the Easter Rising as 'a stab in the back'. Irish POWs in German camps sang 'God save the King' when the Germans argued that they should support the Easter Rebels. There were however other statements of 'Irishness' expressed. Some Connaught Rangers took to serving under a huge green flag, emblazoned with a gold harp. Stephen Gwynn, a member of Parliament for the I.P.P. took leave from the front in 1916 only to be pelted with eggs in his own constituency. Even Redmond, Dillon and Devlin had rallied to the Irish prisoners who were survivors of the Easter Rising, going to the extent of pointing out that no members of the Confederacy in the USA were executed after the American Civil War.

BLACK FRIDAY

At Westminster Lloyd George feared that the Irish situation might destabilise British relations with the USA. To try to settle the Home Rule issue he met with Sir Edward Carson and John Redmond separately. In the interests of the war effort he persuaded Redmond to accept the exclusion of six counties of Ulster for the duration of the Great War only. However, in his meeting with Sir Edward Carson he gave a written assurance that exclusion of the six counties would be permanent. John Redmond was unaware of Lloyd George's pledge to Carson when he called an Ulster Convention in St Mary's Hall Belfast for delegates of the United Irish League (U.I.L.) to discuss temporary exclusion of North-East Ulster from Home Rule. The U.I.L. was essentially the constituency council of the I.P.P. and included influential clergy and business men.

The Ulster Convention was held on 23 July 1916 and was to go down in history as Black Friday. Today Black Friday is virtually forgotten but it was to initiate a division between border Nationalists and East Ulster Nationalists. The U.I.L. argued that Fermanagh, Tyrone, South Armagh and Derry City, unlike counties Antrim and Down, had Catholic majorities and could see no reason why they should be part of a

The front line seems far away from the mind of James McKenna and the 6th Connaught Rangers when this humourous postcard was sent from Co. Cork to Belfast in 1915. It was in November of that year when the regiment left Ireland

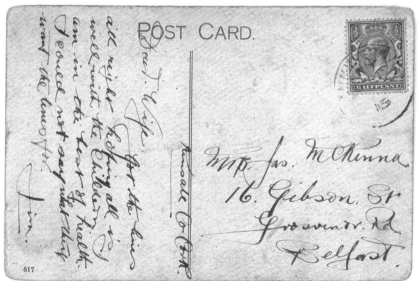

Even though communication with the troops was sometimes difficult, news from home and contact with loved ones was always important to the soldiers at the front line. A missed or lost letter could evoke feelings that they had been forgotten about

Papa chéri, nous sommes bien sages. Maman nous
envoie à l'école et nous pensons toujours à toi !

The postcard translates – 'Dear
Papa, we are learning well.
Mother takes us to school and
we always think of you'. It is
clear from this postcard that
James McKenna was thinking
about his children and perhaps
had the thought that he might
not see them again

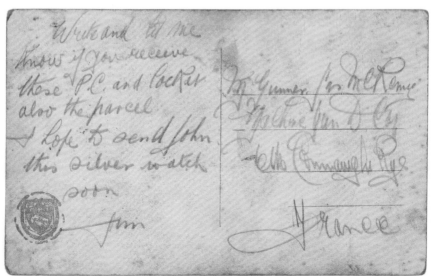

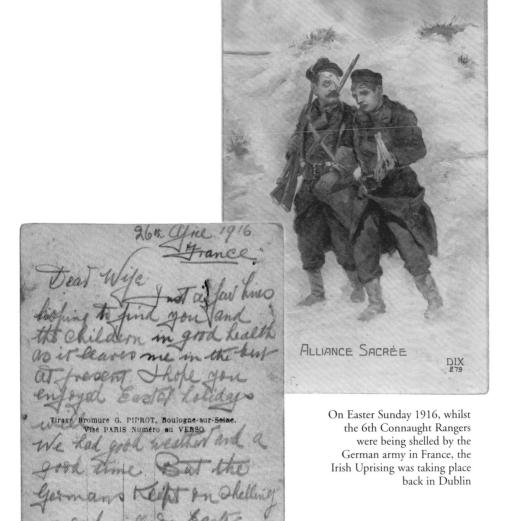

26th April 1916.
France.

Dear Wife
just a few lines
hoping to find you and
the children in good health
as it leaves me in the best
at present. I hope you
enjoyed Easter holidays
well

Tirage Bromure G. PIPROT, Boulogne-sur-Seine.
Visé PARIS Numéro au VERSO

We had good weather and a
good time. But the
Germans kept on shelling
us especially on Easter
Sunday the big shell
dropped close to the
chapel but did not
strike it

ALLIANCE SACRÉE

DIX
279

On Easter Sunday 1916, whilst
the 6th Connaught Rangers
were being shelled by the
German army in France, the
Irish Uprising was taking place
back in Dublin

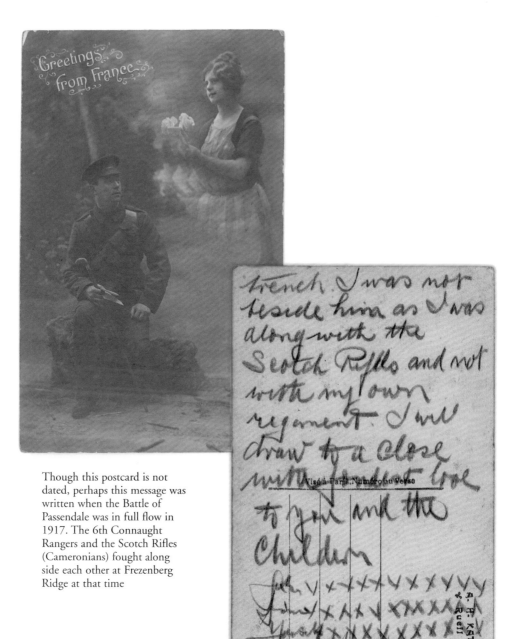

Though this postcard is not dated, perhaps this message was written when the Battle of Passendale was in full flow in 1917. The 6th Connaught Rangers and the Scotch Rifles (Cameronians) fought along side each other at Frezenberg Ridge at that time

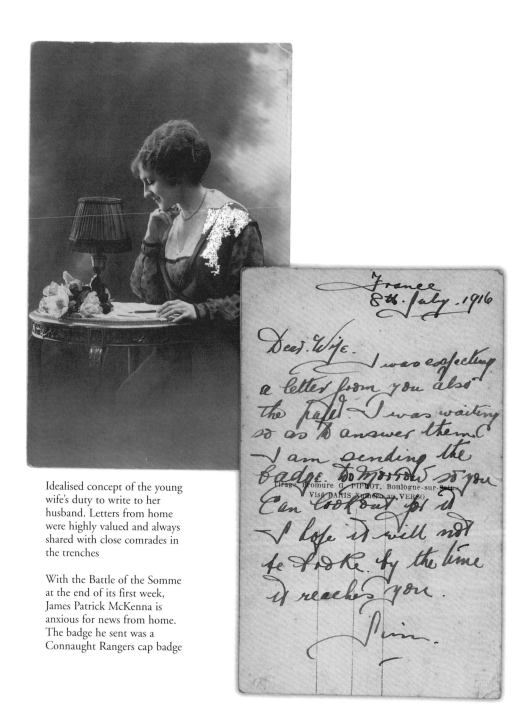

Idealised concept of the young wife's duty to write to her husband. Letters from home were highly valued and always shared with close comrades in the trenches

With the Battle of the Somme at the end of its first week, James Patrick McKenna is anxious for news from home. The badge he sent was a Connaught Rangers cap badge

France
8th. July. 1916

Dear. Wife. I was expecting a letter from you also the paper I was waiting so as to answer them I am sending the badge to morrow so you can look out for it I hope it will not be broke by the time it reaches you.

Jim.

The Virgin Mary and the
Sacred Heart are invoked to aid
an Allied victory. For the
Catholics of the 6th Connaught
Rangers the motivation of
fighting for 'Poor Catholic
Belgium' would have been a
major factor in joining the war

Below: This card was sent along
with a small tin of cigarettes at
Christmas 1915 from Princess
Mary and Friends

A pro-war recruitment postcard

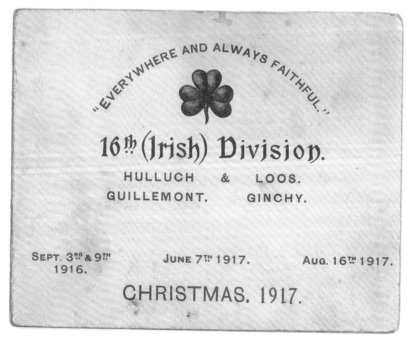

Postcard sent by a Connaught Ranger to his family in Belfast, Christmas 1917

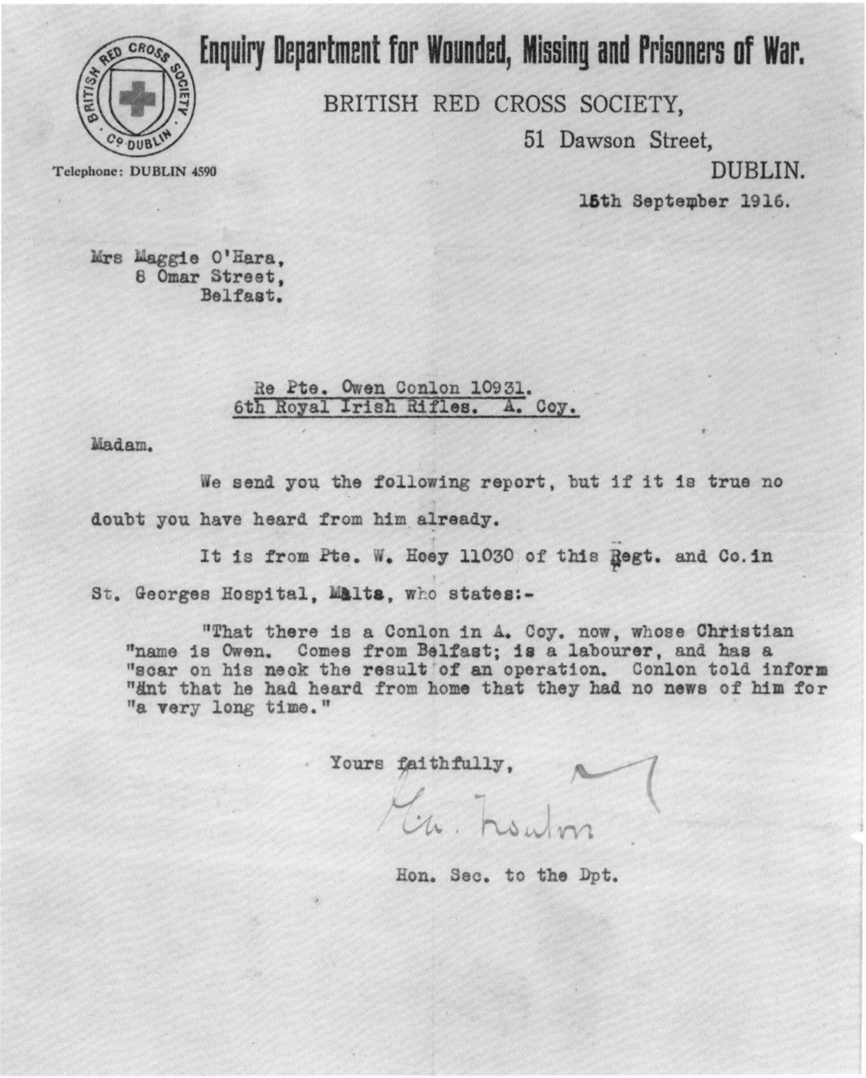

Enquiry Department for Wounded, Missing and Prisoners of War.

BRITISH RED CROSS SOCIETY — Cº DUBLIN

BRITISH RED CROSS SOCIETY,
51 Dawson Street,
DUBLIN.

Telephone: DUBLIN 4590

15th September 1916.

Mrs Maggie O'Hara,
8 Omar Street,
Belfast.

Re Pte. Owen Conlon 10931.
6th Royal Irish Rifles. A. Coy.

Madam.

We send you the following report, but if it is true no doubt you have heard from him already.

It is from Pte. W. Hoey 11030 of this Regt. and Co.in St. Georges Hospital, Malta, who states:-

"That there is a Conlon in A. Coy. now, whose Christian
"name is Owen. Comes from Belfast; is a labourer, and has a
"scar on his neck the result of an operation. Conlon told inform
"ant that he had heard from home that they had no news of him for
"a very long time."

Yours faithfully,

Hon. Sec. to the Dpt.

Owen Conlon was killed 11 months earlier in Gallipoli
at the Battle of Sari Bair, 10th Aug. 1915

TO MY DEAR MOTHER

Un Bonjour de

Mother's Day card from Sgt James
Conlon, 6th Connaught Ranger,
from the front 1917

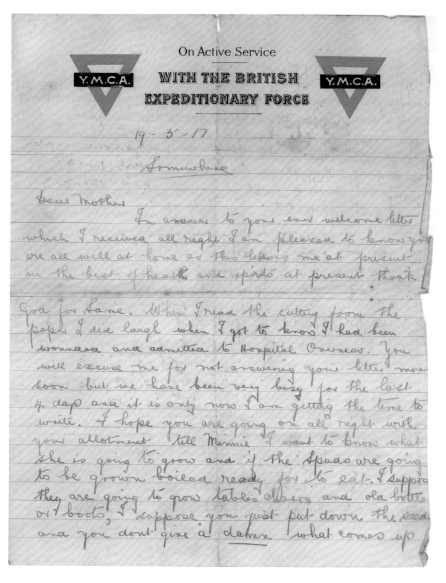

On Active Service

Y.M.C.A. **WITH THE BRITISH** **Y.M.C.A.**
EXPEDITIONARY FORCE

19 - 5 - 17

Somewhere

Dear Mother

In answer to your ever welcome letter which I received all right I am pleased to know you are all well at home as this leaves me at present in the best of health and spirits at present thank God for Same. When I read the cutting from the paper I did laugh when I got to know I had been wounded and admitted to Hospital Overseas. You will excuse me for not answering your letter more soon but we have been very busy for the last 4 days and it is only now I am getting the time to write. I hope you are going on all right with your allotment tell Minnie I want to know what she is going to grow and if the spuds are going to be grown boiled ready for to eat. I suppose they are going to grow tables chairs and old bottle or boots, I suppose you just put down the seed and you dont give a damn what comes up

Letter from Sgt James Conlon, 6th Connaught Rangers, to his mother 1917

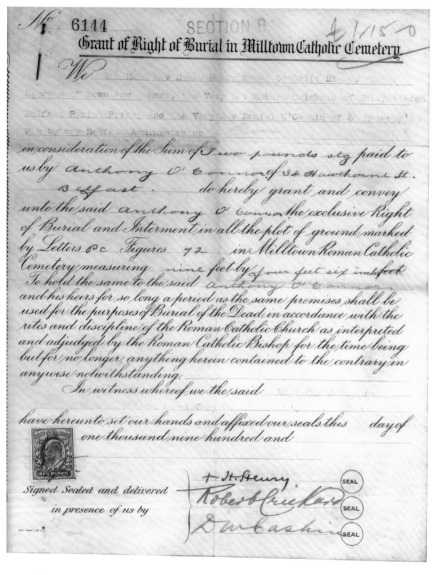

No. 6144 SECTION B. £1/15 0

Grant of Right of Burial in Milltown Catholic Cemetery

We .... John Henry Roman Catholic Bishop ....
.... of Down and Connor, the Very Rev Robert Crickard of ....
Belfast Parish Priest and the Very Rev Daniel M'Cashin of St Joseph's
.... bury Belfast Administrator ....

in consideration of the Sum of *Two pounds stg* paid to
us by *Anthony O'Connor* of *34 Hawthorne St.*
Belfast. do hereby grant and convey
unto the said *Anthony O'Connor* the exclusive Right
of Burial and Interment, in all the plot of ground marked
by Letters & Figures *72* in *Milltown Roman Catholic*
Cemetery measuring *nine* feet by *four feet six inches* feet.
To hold the same to the said *Anthony O'Connor*
and his heirs for so long a period as the same premises shall be
used for the purposes of Burial of the Dead, in accordance with the
rites and discipline of the Roman Catholic Church as interpreted
and adjudged by the Roman Catholic Bishop for the time being
but for no longer, anything herein contained to the contrary in
anywise notwithstanding.
In witness whereof we the said ....

have hereunto set our hands and affixed our seals this .... day of
.... one thousand nine hundred and ....

Signed Sealed and delivered ⎯ + H. Henry   (SEAL)

in presence of us by ⎯ Robert Crickard   (SEAL)

D. M'Cashin   (SEAL)

Grant of Burial in Milltown Cemetery for a grave bought by his uncle to bury Sgt James Conlon, who died after returning home suffering from mustard gas poisoning in 1918. For those casualties who died at the front or whose bodies were never found the War Memorials at the battlefronts are a permanent reminder. For soldiers who died after they were discharged, but who probably died as a direct result of the war, there is no official recognition. This grave in Milltown Cemetery is the resting place of James Conlon who died in a convalescent house in Cushendall in 1918, two weeks after returning to Belfast

This envelope, heavily postmarked, seems to have made its way round the world during the War, unsuccessful as it was at finding its intended recipient James Patrick McKenna. The discovery of McKenna's certificate of transfer from the 6th Connaught Rangers to the 5th Battalion, Royal Irish Fusiliers, where he served as a Lewis Gun Instructor, reveals his regimental number as 30229. It is likely that the most visible address in white was the last to be added and although addressed to 11 Bn Royal Irish Fusiliers it finally found him

Particulars of Service

Date of Enlistment 17th November 1914

Proceeded on Furlough pending transfer to the Army Reserve, or Discharge on _____

Passed medically fit for the Army Reserve on ✓

Due for Transfer to the Army Reserve on ✓

Due for final Discharge on 15th May 1918

Cause of Transfer or Discharge Being No longer physically fit for War Service, para. 392 (XVI) King's Regulations

Campaigns, Medals and Decorations British Ex. Forces France 1915-16-17-18.

Educational and other Certificates, and dates _____

Nil.

WARNING.—If you lose the enclosed Certificate a duplicate cannot be issued.

You should, therefore, on no account part with it or forward it by post when applying for a situation, but should use a copy, attested by a responsible person, for the purpose.

CIVIL EMPLOYMENT.

The National Association for Employment of Ex-Soldiers exists for helping men of good character to obtain employment.

The Head Office is at 119, Victoria Street, London, S.W., and it has numerous branches throughout the Kingdom. The addresses are given in the Guide to Civil Employment, a copy of which is handed to every man of good character on leaving the Colours.

Men who are not already registered for employment should apply to the branch nearest their homes.

D. D. & L., London, E.C.
April W.W 5,000,000 6/15 Sch. 11.
Forms 2. 44929

Army Form B. 2067.

Serial No. 4091

Character Certificate of No. 2583 Rank Sgt. Name James Conlon

Connaught Rangers Regiment,

Born in the Parish of Belfast

near the Town of _____ in the

County of Antrim on the

date 17-6-1891

Trade as stated by him on enlistment Labourer (own)

DESCRIPTION ON LEAVING THE COLOURS.

Height 5 ft 6½ in. Identification Marks:—

Complexion fresh G.S. Wound

Eyes Blue Left Hand.

Hair fair Scar on Both Hand.

Signature of Soldier _____

* To prevent impersonation.

In the event of any doubt arising as to the bona fides of the bearer, the above description and signature should be carefully compared with present appearance and handwriting.

Any Person finding this book, unless it can at once be restored to the Owner, should place it in a Post Office Letter Box for return to:—

THE SECRETARY,

WAR OFFICE,

LONDON, S.W.

ARMY FORM B. 2067 A/A
W.5712. C.A.E.L 7500.

WARNING.—If you lose this Certificate a duplicate cannot be issued.

Army Form B. 2079.

Certificate of discharge of No. 2583 (Rank) Sgt.

(Name) James Conlon

(Regiment) Connaught Rangers

who was enlisted at Belfast

on the 17th November 1914.

He is discharged in consequence of Being No longer physically fit for War Service, paras. 392 (XVI) King's Regulations

after serving 3 years 180 days with the Colours, and _____ years _____ days in the Army Reserve.

(Place) Cork

(Date) 15th May 1918 Signature _____ Officer i/c Records Cork 15th May 1918.

*Description of the above-named man on when he left the Colours.

Age 31 23 yrs Marks or Scars, whether on face or other parts of body.

Height 5 ft 6½ ins. G.S. Wound Left Hand

Complexion fresh Scar on Both Hand

Eyes Blue

Hair fair

*Should agree with the description on Character Certificate, Army Form B. 2067

(4367) Wt.W9712/M3745 800,000 9/15 D.D.& L. Sch. 44. Form/Stn/G54.

N.B.—Any person finding this Certificate is requested to forward it, in an unstamped envelope, to the Secretary, War Office, London, S.W.

The Character here given is based on continuous records of the holder's conduct and employment throughout his military career.

This is to Certify that No. 2583 Rank Sgt. Name James Conlon

has served with the Colours in the Connaught Rangers for 3 years 180/365 years.

An intelligent & hardworking N.C.O.

Signature W.P. Clarke Colonel

Commanding Officer i/c Records Cork

Date 15th May 1918

If further particulars as to his character and record of service are required within three years of above date, apply to _____ where he is registered for civil employment.

* This space is intended to be filled in by any organisation which has registered the man's name and is prepared to supply further information.

Medals in the possessions of the Conlon and Donaghy families. From left to right, in rows, from the top they are:

1. Connaught Rangers cap badge
2. British War Medal (front)
3. British War Medal (back)
4. Royal Irish Rifles cap badge
5. Victory Medal (front)
6. Victory Medal (back)
7. Buttons from the Irish Volunteers uniform of John Conlon, brother of James and Owen
8. 1914–15 Star

Owen Conlon's mother received this 'death penny' from the War Department. Note the error in the spelling, 'Conlan' rather than 'Conlon'. Below: the belt buckle of an Irish Volunteer uniform

partitioned Ireland. The succeeding debates were very acrimonious with those most opposed to Ulster exclusion claiming that the Convention was rigged. Redmond who chaired the meeting threatened to resign if the motion to agree to partition was not passed. Joe Devlin made a forty-five minute speech in which he claimed exclusion would only be temporary and that if the motion was not accepted then the struggle for Home Rule would be greatly set back. Devlin's intervention was decisive and six-county exclusion was accepted by 475 votes to 265. However it was a misleading majority. Those against refused to accept the vote claiming 'Partitionists' had strung out their speeches until the anti-agreement buses had to go.

On 22 July 1916 Lloyd George told Redmond that partition was to be permanent. Redmond felt betrayed and threatened to oppose the Bill at every stage and made a speech in the House of Commons stating that his faith in constitutional methods had been destroyed. In December 1918 John Dillon admitted that since the summer of 1916 the I.P.P. had been 'going downhill at an ever accelerating pace'. The division between East Ulster and West Ulster was complete. Owen Rodgers of the AOH in Fintona, Co. Tyrone, and others like him, were labeled as 'Black Fridayists'. Eamon Phoenix estimated that the split in Northern Nationalism lasted from Black Friday 1916 until at least 1928.

We can only conjecture on the extent of demoralisation among the Irish Volunteers in the Great War from Ulster when the news of Black Friday reached the front.

Those soldiers from the Falls Road who had joined the Connaught Rangers to obtain Home Rule had had their hopes dashed. Far from returning to an Ireland ruled by a 32-County Home Rule Parliament, Nationalist Volunteers were returning to a devolved six-county province where they and their co-religionists would probably be in a state of permanent political powerlessness.

BIBLIOGRAPHY

Belfast Boys: How Unionists and Nationalists fought and died together in the First World War, Richard S. Grayson, Continuum, 2009.

Northern Nationalism: Nationalist Politics, Partition and the Catholic Minority in Northern Ireland 1890–1940, Eamon Phoenix, Ulster Historical Foundation, 1994.

Conceiving Revolution: Irish Nationalist Propaganda and the Great War, Ben Novick, Four Courts Press, 2001.

Catholic Belfast and Nationalist Ireland in the era of Joe Devlin 1871–1934, A. C. Hepburn, Oxford University Press, 2008.

Charles Brett MC: an Irish Soldier with the Connaught Rangers in the Great War, Charles Brett, The Somme Association, 2007.

World War I and the Question of Ulster, The letters of Lilian and Wilfred Spender, Margaret Baguley, Irish Manuscripts Commission, 2009.

The Connaught Rangers Mutiny, India 1920

Siobhán Brennan Deane
and Seán O'Hare

In June 1920 the 1st Battalion of the Connaught Rangers was stationed at Wellington Barracks in Jullundur and at Solon and Jutogh in the Punjab region of British India. These garrisons were in strategic positions between Delhi and Simla and many of the soldiers of the Connaught Rangers who were serving there were experienced veterans of the battlefields of WW1. By the time summer ended in 1920 however, sixty-one of these Rangers would be convicted by army court martial of mutiny, fourteen would be sentenced to death and the remainder imprisoned. Of those who received the ultimate sentence, all but one would be pardoned. It would be 21-year-old Private James Daly of County Westmeath who would be executed on 2nd November 1920 and in so doing would become the last ever soldier in the British Army to be shot for a military offence.

But how did these events unfold and why did the Connaught Rangers mutiny? According to official sources and Belfast newspaper reports at the time, the matter was clear cut: it was the work of Sinn Féin propaganda received by the soldiers from home.[1] The *Irish News* on 5th July 1920 reiterated these sentiments but gives no opinion as to how the news of the mutiny was received by ex-soldiers of the Connaught Rangers in Belfast.

> The whole affair is believed to be concerned with the Sinn Fein agitation and it is hoped the prompt measures of the authorities will cause the men to settle down.

But these views were not shared by the men themselves in India. Both Joseph Hawes and John Flannery, participants in the mutiny in 1920, recalled some years later their own reasons for their actions.[2] Flannery in particular had this to say:

> It has been suggested that the Mutiny was organised and brought to issue by outside influences. This is not so, and readers can judge for themselves the manner in which the trouble was caused in far-off India. The Rangers learned, through actions of the Press, of the strocious [sic] deeds of the Black and Tans in Ireland. This news was later verified by letters which some of the men received from their relatives. Up to that point, the men were happy in the thought that they had played their part in the fight for the liberties and rights of small nations, their own included. But the news from home gave them a great shock. On each

man's face one could soon see the stamp of sorrow and disappointment, and, forthwith, a wave of indignation swept through the barracks.

On 27th June 1920 the men at Jullundur barracks discussed what they should do in protest at events in Ireland and after agreement, early the next day, about 30 men from C Company refused to parade and 'when ordered to do so by the orderly sergeant responded by shouting 'Up the Rebels'.[3] By 9.30 that morning twenty-eight mutineers would be in the guard room.

In the hope that the matter would be dealt with swiftly and quietly, Lieutenant-Colonel Deacon, the Commanding Officer in charge of the Battalion, appealed to the men to abandon their protest and resume duties as normal. According to Hawes, a leader of the rebellion:

> He [Deacon] referred to his service with the Connaughts, 33 years, and to the great history of the Connaughts as fighting soldiers and to their proud flag. He went on to advise us, he was actually crying, to return to our bungalows and the whole matter would be forgotten. He made a very eloquent appeal. I was afraid he might convince the men, so I stepped forward and said 'All the honours in the Connaught flag are for England; there are none for Ireland, but there is going to be one today and it will be the greatest honour of them all.'[4]

The ever changing manner and mood of these unfolding events are highlighted by the fact that two of the mutineers, on hearing the words issued by Deacon, returned to duty whilst a guard in charge of the prisoners, removed his belt and bayonet and asked to be confined with his comrades.[5]

As word of the mutiny spread throughout the Battalion the numbers rallying to the cause began to rise. Official estimates state that by the evening of 28th June 200 men were on protest with this figure rising to 390 just two days later. Approximately 100 men still remained loyal to the British and these were transferred to another unit. With such rising numbers, officials were at a loss as to the appropriate course of action to take and in the short term negotiation seemed the best option. Hence, the mutineers formed a committee of seven members who, with the later approval of the other mutineers decided, according to Hawes,

> that our aims should be to make an open protest to the world against the tactics of the British forces in Ireland. We also decided that order must be kept in the barracks, with the same discipline as if the officers were in charge ... Men were then detailed to put our orders in effect. Guards were placed and material was procured from the Bazaar to make tricolours and inside an hour the tricolour was flying from the flagstaff and several bungalows, and green, white and orange rosettes appeared as if by magic on the men's breasts.[6]

Word was soon sent to the Connaught Rangers stationed at Jutogh and Solon in the hope that they too would join in the protest and in the case of the garrison at Solon this proved fruitful. Private James Daly emerged as spokesman, refusing to take orders until all British soldiers had been withdrawn from Ireland. The Catholic chaplain at Solon, Fr Baker, persuaded the mutineers to give up their weapons and these were placed in the armoury. Feeling that they had made a mistake in giving up their weapons the mutineers decided to retrieve them and under cover of darkness attacked the armoury with fateful consequences. Privates Smythe and Sears were shot and killed by the guards defending and those who took part in the charge were placed under arrest.

Within three days the mutiny was over, the garrisons at Jullundar and Solon were taken over by loyal regiments and those who had mutinied were placed in a makeshift prison. The prisoners eventually transferred to the prison at Dagshai.

After courts martial and subsequent appeals it was only Private Daly who would eventually be executed. It was believed that he had been responsible for the raid on the armoury at Solon and therefore bore responsibility for the deaths of two Connaught Rangers. It was also thought that Daly must be made an example of, as the authorities in India could not let such an incident go unpunished. Anti-British feeling was running high in the country after the massacre of hundreds of Indians at Amritsar in 1919 and if the British could not be seen to maintain control over British troops how could control over Indian soldiers ever be maintained. Lord Chelmsford, the Viceroy of India, remarked,

Connaught Rangers at Jullundur barracks, India. Second right middle row, Pte F. Jordan, from Lurgan, Co. Armagh

we should find ourselves in a position of great difficulty in the future with regard to Indian troops in similar circumstances if, in the case of British soldiers, we did not enforce the supreme penalty where conditions justified it.[7]

The execution of Daly was undertaken by members of the 2nd Battalion of the Royal Fusiliers 'which was posted to Aden immediately after the execution to keep the men out of contact with soldiers from any Irish regiments.'[8]

Prison conditions for the mutineers at Dagshai were severe, though not as severe as they had been in the temporary camp at Jullundur where the Battalion Medical Officer, Dr Philip Carney was so incensed by what he saw he described conditions as 'inhuman' in several reports to

Army Form W.3996

INSTRUCTIONS FOR THE GUIDANCE OF COURTS MARTIAL
WHERE A SENTENCE OF DEATH HAS BEEN PASSED.

To _N° 35178 Private Joseph Hawes_

The Court have found you guilty of the following charges _____
Forming in a mutiny in His Majesty's military forces

_____ but not guilty of the following charges _____

The Court have passed a sentence of death upon you.

The Court have made a ne- recommendation to mercy in the following
terms:

Sentence of death passed on Private Joseph Hawes. Few death sentences were ever reprieved.
(Bureau of Military History, 1913–21. Cathal Brugha Barracks, Dublin)

Higher Command.[9] Shortly before being transferred back to England and the prisons there, Private John Miranda who had been sentenced to two years hard labour, died at Dagshai prison hospital of enteric fever.

In December 1920 the mutineers were taken from Bombay harbour to Southampton and onwards to prisons in England, Scotland and Wales. For those prisoners with longer sentences, their early release would come about as a result of the Anglo-Irish Treaty. This Treaty also meant the end of several Irish regiments, including the Connaught Rangers, whose colours were received back by King George V at Windsor Castle on 12th June 1922. Whilst the link between Irishmen serving in the British military continued, especially during World War Two, the editorial in the *Irish News* on 13th June 1922 summed up many nationalist feelings at the time:

The end of that particular chapter of Anglo-Irish history is written today; it is the report of yesterday's ceremony at Windsor Castle where officers of six 'South of Ireland' regiments handed over their 'colours' to King George V on permanent disbandment.

Five of the regiments concerned had been world famous – some of them for more than two centuries. They were:

The Royal Irish Regiment
The Connaught Rangers
The Munster Fusiliers
The Dublin Fusiliers and The Leinster Regiment
The South Irish Horse were 'raised' during the last war.

Perhaps the Dublin Fusiliers were at all times the most numerous body; but they were not more notable than the Connaught Rangers and the Munster Fusiliers.

The last named Regiment was amongst the first to go into the fight in 1914; one battalion alone lost 180 officers and over 4,000 rank and file in the course of the war. If honest returns were made – and they never were made – it would be found that the five Irish Regiments named left at least 40,000 of their 'strength' on the battlefields of Europe and Asia between 1914 and 1918.

Now the Regiments have vanished. Protests against this disbandment have been published. It was a wise and necessary step. At this moment it is impossible to forsee conditions under which men from Munster, Leinster and Connaught would enlist for service in the British Army again.

All the men of each of these Regiments went forth to fight for 'the rights and liberties of small nations' – including Ireland. They saw their reward at the end of 1918 and during the ghastly 30 months that followed the Armistice.

How many men of the Connaught Rangers who 'mutinied' in India as a protest against Greenwoodism in Ireland still remain in prison cells?

But it is enough to note the disappearance of the Irish Regiments from the Army in which they had been spearheads for more than 200 years. Moralisers can exhaust vocabularies in the effort to 'do justice to the occasion'. In Ireland it is fully realised.

REFERENCES
1   *Belfast Telegraph*, 5th July 1920.
2   Witness statements of Joseph Hawes (WS 262) and John Flannery (WS 287). Bureau of
       Military History, 1913–1921. Cathal Brugha Barracks, Dublin.
3   *The Devil to Pay: The Mutiny of the Connaught Rangers, India, July 1920*, Anthony
       Babington, Pen & Sword Books, 1991, p.7.
4   Joseph Hawes WS262.
5   *The Devil to Pay*, p. 8.
6   Joseph Hawes (WS 262).
7   *The Devil to Pay*, p. 57.
8   Ibid, p. 61.
9   Ibid, p. 26.

Stephen Lally's
Rebel Rangers

Brian Hanley

When Connaught Ranger's mutineer Stephen Lally composed this poem during 1924, he was serving as a soldier in the National (Free State) Army based at Renmore Barracks in Galway. Born around 1900 in the west of Ireland, Lally had joined the British Army as a teenager and fought in the Great War, being wounded at least once. Despite claiming republican sympathies, and some contact with the IRA, he joined the Connaught Rangers in 1919 and was serving in India during 1920, where he took part in the mutiny. Lally asserted that the Mutineers had connections with Indian nationalists and had hoped to spark off a more general rebellion. Jailed in the Mutiny's aftermath, on his release, like several of his colleagues, he joined the Free State Army.

However, when Lally wrote this poem, as part of a memoir of the Mutiny, he was also working as an intelligence officer for the Anti-Treaty IRA. He remained active in the IRA until the 1940s, being commander of its Manchester unit for a period. He returned to Ireland in 1939 and was briefly interned during 1940. He enrolled in the Irish Defence Forces in the later years of the war and was involved in campaigning for the memory of the Mutineers for the rest of his life. Lally was one of the first to record his experiences of the Mutiny and while his poem may lack literary polish, it stands as a memoir written shortly after the events he describes.

Final Letter written by James Daly, executed mutineer. (Bureau of Military History, 1913–21. Cathal Brugha Barracks, Dublin)

The Rebel Rangers

(1)
There was once a Gallant Regiment
of Irish to the core
They fought on many a battle field
For what they did not know
They were told it was for Erin
Its Freedom and its Cause
And that's why the Connaught Rangers
Fought in all of England's Wars.

(2)
It was always England's policy
To bluff the Irish so
And many a Noble Irish Son
Died fighting the Tyrant's Foe
But soon they learned a lesson these Exiles
Yes so True
They answered the Call of Ireland
Before the Red White and Blue.

(3)
It was on the 28th June in the year 1920
That the signal flashed
From over the waves
The Connaughts in Mutiny
For what the Officers asked us all
The reply we soon did give
For Erins Noble Holy Cause
We would sooner die than live.

(4)
The commanding officers Col. Deakin by
name
Was soon upon the scene
He cried just like a little child
To see if we would yield
But his eye wash did not take a trick
With the Connaughts Brave and Bold
For our answer we had given him
We were pledged to the Green, White and
Gold.

(5)
Now the Officers stood chin forward
They did not know what to do
Till one of our own men stepped forward
Like a soldier brave and true
We are not going to molest you
Gentlemen in any way
So pack up your bag and baggage
Your duty is finished today.

(6)
The Officers now lost all control
Of their duties to the Crown
The Flag of the Republic
Was unfurled to the Breeze
The Connaughts now were heart and hand
With their Brothers over the seas
Officers were then elected from the men
In Mutiny
And Orders quickly given to the men
In the Companies.

(7)
Maintain your arms at all Cost
To use in Self Defence
Remember Boys your Irish
Descended from the Celts
If arms are used against you
You can hold your own I know
And show them that your Irish to the core.

(8)
They sent a full Division
They came in Battle array
They were the South Wales Borderers
And the Field Artillery
Likewise the Seaforth Highlanders
And the Black Watch of renown
And also the Machine Gun Corps
All sent to mow us down.

(9)

But the Rangers never wavered
From this pledge to Erin's foes
As they watched the English Blood hounds
Ready to spill their blood
We then got orders to pack up
And proceed down to a Camp
That was wired all around to keep us in
In case the Barracks we'ed take back.

(10)

So off we went full of joy
And singing all the while
The dear old songs of our native land
Brought many a tear and smile
But still we had to cheer up
And not yield to the foe
For we had Declared ourselves Rebels
And had our own work to do.

(11)

Five days they kept us in this Camp
Beneath the Burning Sun
And had us against the Wall
Prepared to shoot us Down
And only for our Chaplain coming on the
scene
We would all of met our doom that Day
At the orders of Major Payne.

(12)

And now before I finish I wish you all to
know
The Trial we got was only Mock
We were judged by Erin's foe
They sentenced fourteen to death
And carried it out on one
The Dearest Comrade that we had
Gave his life in the Cause He Loved.

(13)

Gods Curse be on you England
And Curse you Charles Munroes
You signed the Death of this Man Bold
And carried out your Blow
The Connaughts you remember
And Revenge will be our Cry
Until we have our sweet Revenge
This will always be our Cry.

Signed
Stephen Lally
Ex-Ringleader Connaught Rangers

VOLUNTEERS.

Off to War:
Newspaper reports from the time

Siobhán Deane

There is no better way to engage the mood of any particular moment in history than to read a newspaper printed at the time, and whilst each individual newspaper will have its own agenda or outlook, the facts surrounding any event can usually be gauged.

There are three Belfast-based newspapers which we are all familiar with today, each with its own political agenda or outlook and each reflecting the opinion of its readership and owners. All of these periodicals were in existence at the same time that the 6th Connaught Rangers were being recruited and sent off to war in 1914. Set out below is how the *Irish News*, *Belfast News Letter* and *Belfast Evening Telegraph* reported the events of the 18th and 19th November 1914.

As would be expected from a paper which was widely read and supported by Belfast nationalists, the *Irish News* had the most detailed information on the gathering in St Mary's Hall and the speech by Joe Devlin to those Irish Volunteers who had enlisted; it also gave most page space to the coverage of the men's journey from the Great Northern train station on to Fermoy, Co. Cork.

The *Belfast News Letter*, in contrast a unionist newspaper, had a short article mentioning the gathering in St Mary's Hall and quoted from some of Joe Devlin's speech and the men's journey through Belfast. It, however, saved most of its commentary about these events for its editorial on 20th April, titled 'Nationalists and the War' and 'Nationalist Sedition' which make clear its attitudes toward the actions and motives of the Irish Volunteers and nationalist recruiting in general.

The *Belfast Evening Telegraph* also covered the events in St Mary's Hall, Joe Devlin's speech and the journey of the Irish Volunteers to the train station; it is evident from their commentary that they found these actions positive. It was also the only paper (probably because it was the only one with the facility to do so) to have a photograph of the soldiers as they made their way towards the train station.

The following articles are reproduced in full as they appeared and whilst the basic information is repeated several times, we replicate each piece to show how the same events were reported to each readership and to give us today, an indication as to how the feelings in each community were being reflected and influenced back in 1914.

Spread on previous pages: 500 members of the Belfast Regiment of the Irish National Volunteers march to the Great Northern Train Station and from there to Fermoy, Co. Cork, to undergo training with the new Irish Division, *Belfast Evening Telegraph*, (2nd ed.), 19 Nov. 1914

Irish News
19th November 1914

BELFAST NATIONALISTS AND THE WAR

Send-Off to Members of the Irish Brigade

STIRRING SCENES

Unique & Memorable Gathering in St. Mary's Hall

MR JOSEPH DEVLIN, M.P.

Impressive & Vigorous Address to I.N.V. Soldiers

THE CAUSE OF THE ALLIES

A demonstration unique in the history of Nationalist Belfast took place last evening in St. Mary's Hall, when the members of the Irish National Volunteer Force, Belfast Regiment, who have joined the colours and leave this morning to enter upon their training at Fermoy, Co. Cork, were entrained under the auspices of the Irish Women's Council, Belfast. The hall, which has been the venue of so many notable gatherings and great meetings associated with the National cause, possesses traditions appealing to all who know and appreciate the part played by Belfast Nationalists in the fight for Irish Self-Government. The building, within whose walls some of the most important assemblages of the National character held in the city of Belfast have taken place, was on this occasion the scene of very significant and, indeed, impressive proceedings, eloquently indicative of the new order of things which has followed on the triumph of the Irish cause and the enactment of a measure of Home Rule. Mr Joseph Devlin, M.P., who presided, and met, as he always does in West Belfast with a reception of thrilling enthusiasm, delivered a very striking and powerful address, and struck the keynote of the whole proceedings in this definition of Ireland's position in relation to the world war and his tribute to the valorous example shown by Belfast Nationalists.

The hall was very effectively adorned; and, appropriate to the occasion, the colours of the Allies were prominent in the decorative scheme. On the platform, the drapery comprised the green flag with harp emblem and the Union Jack intertwined, while around the balcony were suspended parti-coloured flags, including Imperial and Irish insignia, with a large Union Jack as the centre piece. Guards of the I.N.V. in uniform and with rifles and bayonets were in attendance, and gave the proper military touch to the general aspect of the proceedings. The flag of the Belfast Regiment, I.N.V, surrounded by a special guard of honour, was borne prominently on the platform, where the members of the Pipers' Band, in Gaelic costume, and with a Red Hand standard, added to the picturesque elements in the scene. The main body of the hall was occupied by long tables, at which eight hundred guests – the men who have joined the colours – were seated. They were as fine, smart, and soldierly body of men as one could find anywhere, and commanded the admiration of the military men whose khaki uniforms distinguished them amongst the assemblage of representative citizens and prominent clergy on the platform.

MR. DEVLIN'S ADDRESS
Belfast Nationalists' Example to All Ireland

Mr Joseph Devlin M.P., who was received with loud and prolonged cheering said – This function to-night is at once unique and significant. I am delighted to have the opportunity of saying a few words to my friends, comrades, and constituents on their departure to take up their training for service under the colours in the great war now being waged on the Continent. I have had occasion time and again in all my public associations with all the Nationalists and Catholics of our city to admire their spirit of self-sacrifice, their fight for principles which they hold dear, their courage and determination in face of difficulty and danger, and their unstinted and generous support of every good and great cause. (Cheers) I confess I never felt prouder of them, and I am deeply moved by the present manifestation of patriotic spirit exhibited by the 700 young men who have

PLUCKILY AND SPONTANEOUSLY RESPONDED TO THE CALL OF DUTY

in the nation's hour of difficulty and trial. (Cheers) Nationalist Belfast has always shown an example in translation into practical action the needs of the hour. You have never failed in any emergency or trial in the past. You have not failed on the present occasion. (Cheers) I have asked no man to volunteer as an individual; I have applied no pressure in any shape or form to any man associated with the National Volunteers in Belfast. (Hear, hear) I have merely pointed out the duty of the young men of Ireland in relation to the present war. I have told them that on the side of the Allies there lies justice, right, principle, and freedom. (Cheers) I have explained that Mr Redmond and the Irish Party have given pledges and assurances to the British democracy that if justice were given to Ireland, if her Legislature were restored, and if Irishmen were allowed to govern themselves in their own land, then Ireland would loyally act as a free partner in the confines of Empire, and by the Empire they would stand or fall. (Cheers) Well, we have seen the Home Rule Bill placed on the Statute Book. We have succeeded in making National Self Government the law of the land. The democracy of Great Britain has stood faithfully by us to the last. Are we in these circumstances to prove false to our promises, and recreant to our pledges and our solemn obligations? (Cries of 'No!') We stand for all practical purposes in the position of the Boers in South Africa. (Cheers) What a splendid example General Louis Botha and his brave followers are exhibiting at the present moment. No country fought more heroically for its right for the hearths and homes of the men of the Veldt than the South African Boer. But at the conclusion of the war, when a treaty of peace was signed and when the Boers were given their legislation constitution, they declared themselves

AS FREE AND LOYAL CITIZENS OF THE BRITISH EMPIRE,

and in the first war which has overtaken the British people since, they have come forward prepared to make every sacrifice and spill their blood in defence of their promises and pledges and the solemn rights guaranteed by the 'scrap of paper' which confers on them the title of free men. (Cheers) The Nationalists of Ireland sympathised with the Boers during the South African War because they felt convinced that they had justice on their side. (Hear, hear.) It was an unpopular stand for the Nationalists of Ireland to take at the time, and it was anything but in their interests to do so. But we never counted the cost where principle was involved, and, just as then we now range ourselves on the side of honour, truth, and principle. (Cheers) I am proud beyond measure at the fine example which the Belfast Nationalist Volunteers have given to Ireland: in conjunction with every Belfast man, I shall watch the career of this battalion of the Irish Brigade with feelings of pride, hope and confidence. (Hear, hear) I am satisfied they will sustain the splendid traditions not only of their city, but to their country and their race for valour, for honour, for chivalry, and, as units in an army stand for all we value highest in civilisation – religion and progress. I am satisfied that the young men of the National Volunteers of Belfast who have

SO COURAGEOUSLY VOLUNTEERED FOR ACTIVE SERVICE
AT THIS MOMENTOUS AND ARRESTING MOMENT

when the fate and future of human liberty are threatened, will emulate the example of their forefathers who fought with so much renown and fame in the Irish Brigade in the service of France in the very locality where the centre of the struggle is now being so gallantly defended by the army of the Allied forces. (Cheers) I salute the members of the present contingent on their departure in a spirit of pride and gratitude. I know they will prove worthy of their city and their friends, and, when the history of the present war comes to be written and viewed in the true perspective, the Nationalists of Belfast will ever regard with feelings of generous pride the fact that from the capital of the North of Ireland their brothers and comrades showed an illustration of patriotism and courage worthy to rank with the noble deeds and inspiring efforts of the men who made McCracken's city famous in the struggle for Irish liberty over a century ago. (Loud cheers) May every good fortune, success, and blessing attend the colours of the Irish National volunteers of Belfast, most of whom are from my own constituency of West Belfast, whose safe return, crowned with the laurels of glory worthily earned in the arena of a great conflict on behalf of a righteous cause, will bring joy to the hearts of all our fellow-citizens. (Loud cheers)

Irish News
20th November 1914

OFF TO FERMOY

Belfast Recruits for Irish Brigade

WONDERFUL SCENES

Crowds of Thousands Witness the Departure

The departure of six hundred men of the Irish National Volunteers – the first contingent from Belfast – to Fermoy for their training, after joining the colours, was attended by quite remarkable scenes yesterday morning. Probably the spectacle was such as has never been witnessed in the streets of Belfast before. Headed by pipers in Gaelic costume, flourishing banners emblazoned with the Red Hand of the O'Neill and distinctively Irish National devices and mottoes, the men marched through Belfast with their khaki-clad officer to the inspiring airs that are inseparably associated with Irish traditions and Ireland's age-long fight for freedom. 'O'Donnell Abu' and 'Clare's Dragoons' resounded in Royal Avenue and Donegall Place as the men swung through the centre of the city to entrain at the Great Northern Railway Station on their long journey southwards. For the present all the men are attached to that famous corps the Connaught Rangers, but it is possible that some may be later on attached to one or other of the equally noted regiments constituting the modern Irish Brigade which is entering into existence, with every recruit full of the desire to emulate the deeds performed on the plains of Belgium and France by that other history-making Irish Brigade two hundred years ago.

Belfast Nationalists have given a fine lead in this critical and momentous period, and it was fitting that such public enthusiasm as was witnessed yesterday should attend the sending off of the first body of brave and stalwart men from this city to swell the ranks of the Irish Brigade. That they will do credit to the community which they represent and bring honour to their city could not be doubted by any person who was present at yesterday's wonderful demonstration and observed the demeanour and bearing of the new soldiers. Though as yet unprovided with uniforms, they presented the smart appearance and marched with the regularity which betokened experience of the drill instructor, while they were manly, well-set-up types drawn from varying grades of society, but all possessing the qualities which come within the true definition of the term 'soldierly.' There was no lavish display of bunting such as marked the departure of other contingents of troops from the city, but if anything was lacking in externals of this particular kind, nothing could exceed the effectiveness of the manifestation of public feeling attendant on the event.

From Henry Place, the entrance to the Victoria Barracks, all the way to the Great Northern Railway Station through the centre of the city – a distance of about a mile –

thousands and thousands of people were congregated, at some points with such density as to necessitate the suspension of traffic. For hours they waited the opportunity of seeing the men march past, and giving them a parting cheer, but though the time of waiting was long the multitude of onlookers increased instead of diminishing, and when at last the music of the pipes and a roll of cheering heralded the approach of the advance guard the streets were packed all the way, and every window had its bunch of onlookers.

The men, who had assembled in the barracks at 7 a.m. and breakfasted there, were later on paraded in the square and sized off into companies by the officers of the Connaught Rangers in attendance, with the assistance of the local Volunteer officer. Having been formed into companies, the men were provided with the first part of their equipment – namely, greatcoats, and about half-past ten o'clock marched off to the railway station. They were under the command of Major Buler, Lieutenant Wickham, and Lieutenant Telford (Connaught Rangers) with some seven or eight non-commissioned officers of that corps, and were accompanied by five bands – the Clann Uladh Pipers' Band, the O'Neill Pipers' Band, the Mandeville Flute Band, and the National Volunteer Bugle Band.

The scenes along the route to the railway station were very striking, the deep fringe of onlookers stretching the entire distance, while cheer after cheer and the waving of hats and handkerchiefs marked the progress of the men who marched along to the martial and stirring music of Irish National airs. It was a rare spectacle for the average citizen and created quite a sensation, the music of the bands causing people to flock from all points to add to the crowd already thronged along the streets. The railway station was completely surrounded by an immense crowd and even the tops of the adjoining sheds were crowded. Immense enthusiasm greeted the arrival at the terminus of Mr. Joseph Devlin, M.P., almost simultaneously with the first batch of the men, but the general public were restricted to Glengall Street and Great Victoria Street, the precincts of the station being guarded by a body of Royal Irish Rifles, while there was also a force of police in attendance under District-Inspector Redmond. A great number, however, of those most intimately connected with the men were admitted and soon the main platform from which the train was to start was crowded from end to end. Mr Samuel Young the veteran M.P. was amongst those present, while the Right Rev. Mgr. O'Doherty, P.P. V.F, Omagh; Rev. T. McCotter, Adm., St Joseph's; Rev. A. Greaven. B.A., C.C., St Paul's; Rev. H. Murray C.C., St. Mary's; and Rev. John McLaverty. C.C., St. Patrick's, the military chaplain in Belfast, were also noticed on the platform, in addition to a very large gathering of public representatives and other prominent citizens.

While the men were entraining the bands played 'God Save Ireland' and 'A Nation Once Again', and 'God Save the King' was sung, while a vigorous rendering of the Belfast Celtic 'war song' also echoed through the station. Before the departure of the train many touching scenes of parting were witnessed, the relatives of the men handing them little gifts, which mostly took the form of rosaries and religious emblems, while cigarettes, sweets, newspapers, etc., were lavishly distributed through the packed carriages constituting the long troop train. Mr Joseph Devlin, M.P., who was cheered to the echo, made his way along the train and took a personal farewell with every individual recruit. Ultimately the final words of command were given, the officers swung into their compartments and to the strains of 'God Save Ireland' and another prolonged cheer the train steamed off, every window framing a crowd of eager and lively faces.

THE MEN REACH FERMOY

Cheered to Quarters by Crowd With Bands

Our Cork Correspondent wires last night:

The news that six hundred of the National Volunteers from Belfast were to arrive in Fermoy to-night spread like wildfire throughout the town, with the consequent result that a demonstration of enthusiastic young men and women assembled at the railway station to accord their Northern friends a right royal reception. The Cross Street National Band, the Barrack Hill Band, and the Pipers' Band turned out from their respective quarters and marched to the Volunteer Drill Hall, from which, after a short time, the several bands, accompanied by the local Volunteers, paraded the town and thence to the station. There could not have been less than 2,000 persons present, and these waited patiently for the arrival of the train which steamed in at 9.20. The men were received by General Miles and Brigadier-General Pickard, the Chairman and members of the Urban Council, officers of the Volunteers, and Rev. M. O'Connell, chaplain of the Brigade, and within a short time the Belfast men were formed up in companies.

THE MEN SHOWED THEY WERE WELL DRILLED

They looked fit, and immediately made themselves quite at home. On their march through the station premises the local Volunteers formed a guard of honour, the immense crowd cheering, whilst the soldiers sang 'It's a long way to Tipperary'. The men were accompanied by the three bands into the new barrack square where a most enthusiastic scene took place with bands playing and the Volunteers cheering, whilst the men of the Royal Irish and Connaught Rangers joined in the reception. General Miles was delighted at the appearance of the men, who, he is sure, will be a credit to the army. The men had everything prepared for them on their arrival and took up their quarters as if they were stationed there all their lives.

THE ARRIVAL AT DUBLIN

The Press Association says:

Five hundred National Volunteers who left Belfast yesterday morning to join the army passed through Dublin yesterday afternoon. They were met by friends at Kingsbridge Station, where tea and cigarettes were provided. The men then proceeded by special train to Fermoy.

The Belfast News Letter
Thursday, 19th November 1914

THE IRISH NATIONAL VOLUNTEERS

LEAVE-TAKING IN BELFAST

Speech by Mr J Devlin, M.P.

There was a large attendance at an entertainment given in St Mary's Hall last night in honour of the members of the Irish National Volunteer Force who have enlisted in the new Army, and who are to leave Belfast to-day to join the regiments to which they have been posted.

Mr Joseph Devlin, M.P. addressing the recruits, and said he was deeply moved by the manifestation of patriotic spirit exhibited by the 700 young men who had pluckily and spontaneously responded to the call of duty in the nation's hour of difficulty and trial. Nationalist Belfast had always shown an example in translating into practical action the needs of the hour. They had never failed in any emergency or trial in the past, and they had not failed on the present occasion. He had asked no man to volunteer as an individual; he had applied no pressure in any shape or form to any man associated with the National Volunteers in Belfast; he had merely pointed out the duty of the young men of Ireland in relation to the present war. He had told them that on the side of the Allies there lay justice, right, principle, and freedom. He had explained that Mr Redmond and the Irish Party had given pledges and assurances to the British democracy that if justice was given to Ireland, if her Legislature were restored, and if Irishmen were allowed to govern themselves in their own land, then Ireland would loyally act as a free partner in the confines of the Empire, and by the Empire they would stand or fall. He would watch the career of the Belfast battalion of the Irish Brigade with feelings of pride, hope, and confidence. He was satisfied they would sustain the splendid traditions not only of the city, but of their country and their race for valour, for honour, for chivalry, and as units of an army stand for all they valued highest in civilisation – religion and progress. He was satisfied that the young men of the National Volunteers of Belfast who had courageously volunteered for active service at this momentous and arresting moment, when the fate and future of human liberty were threatened, would emulate the example of their forefathers who fought with so much renown and fame in the Irish Brigade in the service of France in the very locality where the centre of the struggle was now being so gallantly defended by the army of the Allied Forces.

On the suggestion of Mr. Devlin, it was resolved to send a telegram to the Prime Minister and Mr. John Redmond assuring them 'that the British democracy having conceded Ireland's claim to be incorporated as a free, self-governing community in the British Empire, may count on the Home Rulers of this city to the last man in defence of our common rights and liberties now threatened by Germany'.

The Belfast News Letter
Friday, 20th November 1914

NATIONALISTS AND THE WAR

(EDITORIAL)

While we are pleased to see that about five hundred Nationalist Volunteers have enlisted, we think it right to say that the Unionists do not and cannot accept the conditions on which they have done so, as explained in a telegram from Mr Devlin to the Prime Minister and Mr Redmond. It is right that there should be no misunderstanding on this point now, so that when the war is over, and the Home Rule Act has been repealed, there may be no charges of breach of faith, or at least no excuse for them. We have no objection to his statement that the Army is fighting for the rights of small nationalities and the vindication of human freedom, for Great Britain's declaration of war was primarily due to Germany's invasion of Belgium, while Russia came into it in defence of Serbia, and these are two of the smaller nations in Europe. It may be thought that the Nationalists, like the other people of the United Kingdom, should find in the great question at issue sufficient reason for taking their part in the war without imposing selfish and partisan conditions; but that is not their view. Just as Mr Redmond refused to say a word in support of the Empire until he was paid his price, so the Nationalist Volunteers decline to assist it to fight its battles except on the understanding that the Dublin Parliament shall rule over the whole country. The rights of smaller nationalities and the vindication of human freedom are nothing to them unless associated with the power to tyrannise over the Unionists of Ireland, and especially of Ulster. The member for West Belfast give the Prime Minister 'an assurance that the British democracy, having conceded Ireland's claim to be incorporated as a free self-governing unit of the British Empire, may count on the Home Rulers of this city to the last man in defence of our common rights and liberties now threatened by Prussian militarism'. We assume that the object of the telegram was to place on record for future use the condition on which the Nationalist Volunteers have enlisted. It is a condition however, which has been made by the Nationalists, but not accepted by the electors, the Unionist Party, or even the Government. The British democracy has not conceded the Nationalist claim. In 1886 and 1895 it rejected it, and it has had no opportunity of deciding on the merits of the Bill which has been put on the Statute Book by unconstitutional means. Both the Government and the Nationalists knew that if the Bill had been submitted to the people they would have rejected it, and that is why they took advantage of the great Imperial crisis to pass it without their consent. No action is strong enough to condemn their action, and it is very rash for them to assume that it will be condoned. The electors have not conceded the Nationalist claim and the Unionist Party has declared that when it comes into power it will not allow the Act to stand. Therefore, if the Nationalists will not enlist because the war is just, or because they wish to join in the defence of themselves and their families against a German invasion, they should not do so because they have got Home Rule, for they have not got it. There is no treaty, agreement, or understanding of any kind whatever. Mr Asquith has no power to bind his successors, and the Unionists have given public notice in the clearest terms of their intention. It is necessary to say this much lest anyone should suppose that the Unionists of Ulster have changed their attitude, or that they will change it. But, at the same time, we hope that the Nationalists, putting aside all partisan conditions, will enlist in large numbers, and show that they are as ready as other Irishmen to fight in a good cause. Mr Devlin, in his telegram to the Prime Minister, put the number enlisting in Belfast at a thousand, or twice the correct figure, but doubtless he has influence enough to obtain the other 500 recruits. We notice that the 'Daily Chronicle' had a bitter attack on a body of the Ulster Volunteers because while on a route march they played 'The Boyne Water,' but we are sure it will not have a word of complaint about the Nationalist Volunteers who yesterday played 'A Nation Once Again' 'The Wearin' of the Green' and other Nationalist airs – not on a route march, but in the Victoria Barracks, the property of the Crown. But the Radical newspapers have no sense of fairness. They are determined to hate and malign Ulstermen, and they will continue to do it no matter how often their misrepresentations and inventions are exposed. We do not think the Unionists will much object to Nationalists playing their Party tunes if they are thereby induced to contribute their proportion of new recruits. Every stimulus is needed, for it is two months since the Bill which was to create a boom in recruiting was passed, and very few of them have enlisted.

The Belfast News Letter
Friday, 20th November 1914

NATIONALIST SEDITION

(EDITORIAL)

The publication of seditious newspapers and leaflets by some of the Nationalist factions continues, and the Government is not interfering. Perhaps it accepts Mr. Redmond's assurance that the persons who are responsible are only a few cranks, but the recruiting figures show that the seditious campaign is more effective than anything which the Nationalist leaders are doing. At a time when the Prime Minister states that every man who is fit for military service is needed Nationalist writers revile the British Army, and urge Irishmen to refuse to join it, without running any risk of punishment. Lord Mayo called the attention of the House of Lords to the subject yesterday, but the Government treated the matter with indifference. At a time when a strict censorship is exercised over loyal newspapers which are as anxious as any member of the Government can be for the success of the Allies, rebel newspapers seem free to publish what they like. There is not a country in the world which would tolerate several of the rags that appear regularly in Ireland. Lord Desart informed the House that a short time ago a motor car covered three counties distributing leaflets of a seditious character, and the Government had done nothing, although the name of the owner of the car had been sent to it. He commented on the inaction of the Government, in view of the insufficiency of the response made to Mr Redmond's appeal for recruits. The Earl of Meath alluded to the report that much of the disloyal literature comes from America, but if this is true it must be prepared and sent by those Irish-Americans who were to be made friends of England by the enactment of the Home Rule Bill. But even if the literature is Fenian in its origin, it is circulated in this country by people who are known to the police. Have the authorities given an instruction that all such offences are to be ignored? Perhaps Mr. Birrell had decided that nothing should be done pending the appointment of Mr. Redmond as Irish Prime Minister. It is not surprising that Lord Meath has come to the conclusion that 'in Ireland today no one is responsible for anything at all.' His suggestion that the mines were laid on the Irish coast by German agents by means of ships engaged in the Irish fisheries is one which Lord Crewe says the Government has not heard, but he said it would interest the Admiralty. The persons who write and circulate the seditious newspapers to which we are referring and those who support them, are quite capable of assisting the enemy to lay mines in the trade routes. If they could blow up a British warship, or even British Merchant vessels, they would not care how many lives were lost. One of these periodicals which has been sent to us by a correspondent is full of anti-British articles, letters and paragraphs. One writer rejoices that 'England's robber grip is loosening before the onslaughts of European power,' another hopes that the Kaiser's sailors will gain many such victories as that in the Pacific, while a third urges the Provisional Committee of the Nationalist Volunteers to strike at England now when she is in peril. When Great Britain, the Empire, the Army and the Navy are reviled, it is natural that Ulster should be regarded with special bitterness, and so we find in one of these rebel newspapers a number of libels on the Ulster Volunteers. Ulstermen are not recognised as Irishmen, but are called West Britons, because of their loyalty; and yet the Government has treated them with the greatest injustice in the hope of conciliating the men who are now actively engaged in an anti-recruiting campaign. The betrayal of Ulster has failed to accomplish its object, as everyone not altogether ignorant of Ireland knew that it would, for the Nationalist Volunteers are not recruiting, and the hatred of England remains as strong as ever. The Radical newspapers in England ignore all the evidence of Nationalist disloyalty, but the electors are learning something about it, and it will not make them more disposed to approve of Home Rule when they get the opportunity of pronouncing judgement upon it.

Belfast Evening Telegraph
19th November 1914

FOR IRISH BRIGADE

Send-off to Belfast Men

Address by Mr. J Devlin. M.P.

The smoker and farewell concert promoted by the Irish Women's Council, of which Mrs E. A. Letts, University Square, Belfast, is the esteemed president, which was given in St. Mary's Hall, Belfast, last evening, to about 500 of the Irish National Volunteers (Belfast Regiment), who have enlisted in answer to the country's call for the Irish Brigade, and who leave for training at Fermoy today, was fittingly enthusiastic, and gave a clear indication of the spirit of patriotism which has, especially more recently, been exhibited in regard to recruiting for Kitchener's Army. It afforded indisputable proof that there exists a very strong determination to make the appeals of Irish leaders as successful as they themselves would wish, and throughout the proceedings there was to be noted a keen desire to emphasise the feeling that at this stage in the country's history the response of the men of the North should be unanimous. The large hall was crowded, and some 300 nurses in uniform formed a distinctly picturesque forefront seated on the platform. The building was nicely decorated, a large Union Jack in the background being conspicuous. After a meat tea, during which the Belfast Pipers' Band rendered a number of patriotic selections, the audience heartily joining in with vocal accompaniment.

Mr. Joseph Devlin, M.P. who was given a rousing reception, took the chair. The chairman expressed his delight at presiding over that most interesting and unique function, and at having the opportunity of saying a few words to his friends, comrades and constituents, on their departure for training under the colours for the great war being waged on the Continent. He had occasion, he said, time and again during his long and varied association with the Nationalists of that city to admire their spirit of self-sacrifice, the fight for principle which they had made, and the courage and determination with which they had unstintedly and unwaveringly given their support to all the great national causes. (Cheers). He never felt prouder or more deeply moved than he was that night at the manifestation of splendid manhood, courage, and patriotic spirit exhibited by nearly 700 of the young men of Nationalist Belfast who had come there spontaneously in response to the call of duty to serve the nation in its hour of trial. (Cheers.) Nationalist Belfast has always shown an example in translating into practical form the need of the hour: they had never failed in the hour of trial to do their duty in every emergency that arose, and when he looked round the hall and watched that inspiring scene – which was to him one of the most cheering and glorious sights he had ever witnessed – then he said young Belfast was just as brave as ever it was. (Cheers) During the past few months he had made many speeches in Belfast and Ulster, and he had never asked a single individual to volunteer for the front: he had applied no pressure in any shape or form on any man associated with the Volunteers of that great city. (Cheers.) He had, as he was bound to do, pointed out the duty of the young men of Ireland in relation to the present war. He had told them, and he repeated that night with all the feeling of his heart, that when they went to fight in this great battle on that Continent they went to fight for freedom and for humanity. (Cheers.) Many a time he had pleaded the cause of humanity, of freedom, of justice and right, but there never was a nobler cause of freedom and justice and right than that for which they were going out to fight. (Cheers.) They were doing more, however, than giving their support in the cause of freedom and humanity; they were keeping their pledge of honour to the British democracy. (Cheers.) He had given a pledge to the people of England that if they gave Ireland her freedom and restored to that old nation her long lost Legislature and allowed them to bring into play that God-given genius for self government, then in no part of the world would they have more loyal comrades than the contented and free people of Ireland. (Cheers.) The people of England had placed the Home Rule Bill on the Statue Book, they had made national self government the law of the land, the democracy of Great Britain had stood loyally by them, and those present that night were there to carry out their part of the contract. (Cheers.) They would watch the career of the Irish Brigade with feelings of pride, of hope, and confidence that they would sustain the splendid traditions not only of the city of Belfast, but of the country and of their race for honour and chivalry. When the war was over, and when its story came to be written, they would remember with pride and gratitude that the Nationalists of Belfast had given an illustration of patriotism and courage worthy to rank with the noble deeds and inspiring efforts of the men who made McCracken's city famous over a century ago. (Cheers.) 'Let me hope' continued Mr Devlin, 'that when you are away fighting for freedom that we will take example from the practical precepts you have placed before us.' In conclusion, he thanked in a special degree Mrs Letts who, although differing in religion from 99 percent of those present, had attached herself to the people's cause, and had no other desire than to serve the poor. He also mentioned that he had despatched telegrams to Mr Asquith and Mr Redmond telling them of the response of the Nationalists of Belfast had made to the call of duty.

Other speakers addressed the gathering and musical items were contributed.

Belfast Evening Telegraph
(19th November 1914 later edition)

FOR IRISH DIVISION

I.N.V. Men Leave Belfast

REMARKABLE BARRACK SCENES

The members of the Belfast Regiment of the Irish National Volunteers who enlisted in Lord Kitchener's Army within the past few days, left the city this forenoon bound for Fermoy, County Cork, to undergo training with the new Irish Division.

They mustered about five hundred strong, and were given a farewell from their friends and sympathisers that certainly lacked nothing in fervour and enthusiasm.

The contingent was early at Victoria Barracks, where they paraded on the square at seven o'clock. The men were provided with a substantial breakfast and the time intervening till their departure for the station was occupied with the roll call and other preliminaries, while each man was provided with a greatcoat. The barracks and its environs were the scene during the forenoon of some rather unusual spectacles. From an early hour dense crowds thronged Henry Place and Clifton Street waiting to give the men a hearty send-off, while the rigidity of military discipline relaxed to the extent of concession of admitting the Nationalist bands who came to play the recruits to the station into the barrack interior.

There was no lack of musical accompaniments to the parade preliminaries. Kilted pipers in picturesque Gaelic costume, with their bright-hued banners, lent a touch of colour to the scene, and the Belfast garrison headquarters resounded all the forenoon to the skirl of the pipes, the rattle of the drum, and the call of the bugle from civilian and not from the military combinations.

The bands in attendance were Clann Uladh, O'Neill Pipers, Volunteer Buglers, St Malachy's Hibernian Temperance, and Mandeville Fife and Drum, and they paraded the square in turn to the strains of 'A Nation Once Again,' 'The Wearin' of the Green,' and other Nationalist airs, with 'Tipperary' by way of a variety.

The men appeared to be in the best of spirits, and during a lull in the music gave vent to their exuberance of feeling by lustily declaring in chorused unison that 'Belfast Celtic would be there' – whether at Berlin or at the head of the Irish League was not explained.

Headed by the Clann Uladh Pipers playing 'God Save Ireland', the recruits left the barracks at 10.20, and their progress through the city was accomplished with some difficulty by reason of the eagerness of the crowds in waiting to join the ranks. Mill girls were present in their hundreds and made the air lively with their cheering and singing. The march was via Clifton Street, Donegall Street and Royal Avenue, and the gathering of the Nationalist Volunteers not unnaturally attracted a great deal of public attention, while there was not a little curiosity as to the character of the turnout.

There was another dense throng outside the Great Northern terminus, which the Volunteers reached about a quarter to eleven. Admission to the station was barred except to the travelling public, and inside a guard of the Royal Irish Rifles formed a cordon near the barrier. So great was the crowd that it was only with difficulty the men pushed their way into the station, which they entered by the Glengall Street side, and it was almost an hour before the train, due to leave at eleven, cleared from the station. There was an animated scene on the platform, to which the pipers were admitted.

Mr J. Devlin, M.P. was present and went from carriage to carriage taking a personal leave-taking of every man. Alderman Moore, Councillor M'Entee, Dr Blewitt, Mr Martin J. Bourke, a number of Catholic clergy, and other prominent Belfast Nationalists were also in attendance. The train steamed out at 11.40, amid hearty cheering.

The men will be attached to some of the new battalions of the Connaught Rangers, Leinster Regiment, and the Royal Irish Regiment. Major Buler travelled from Fermoy to take charge of the party, and was accompanied by Lieutenants Telford and Wickham, and by a number of non-commissioned officers. Colonel the Hon. Arthur Hill-Trevor superintended the departure arrangements at the station.

Family Stories

Michael and Robert Brennan

Siobhán Brennan Deane

Michael Brennan and his brother Robert were the two youngest surviving children of Joseph and Kate Brennan who lived in the Carrickhill district of Belfast. This nationalist family had lived in the city since the 1850s. There were nine children but only two, Michael and Robert, enlisted to serve in the British Army and to fight in the Great War. Joining together at Clifton Street Hall on 12th November 1914 they were ordered to serve with the Connaught Rangers; their service numbers were 2496 and 2497.

Of the two brothers Robert, a married man with two young children, was the eldest by three years. Michael, my grandfather, was aged 19. It was not until 1921 that he met and married my grandmother, Mary Catherine Quinn from the Sailortown area of Belfast. It was always known in the family that granda had fought in World War One but it was a topic that was not talked about often. Like others of his generation and nationalist background, such discussions were usually among those who had shared the experience; family were to be protected from the more gory details of warfare. In more recent years when the matter was discussed amongst his children and grandchildren there was a certain realisation and quiet pride in the fact that Michael had fought in the only regiment of the British Army known to have mutinied against how Britain treated its Irish subjects. There was even greater pride in the fact that Michael actually refused his war medals, returning them to the War Office

Michael Brennan

in London in 1923. The more the family learned about his time in the Great War the more they realised that he was a man of some principle.

The exact reasons why Michael and his brother joined the army in 1914 is lost to time; his death in 1979 preceded the enquiring minds of his grandchildren who now regret that they did not have a chance to ask more. But this lack of first-hand knowledge does not mean we cannot make certain informed assumptions. His actions over 90 years ago can be assessed with the benefit of hindsight and using contemporary sources such as local newspapers, the War Office Index Cards and Medal Rolls as well as the Connaught Rangers War Diaries, an insight in to his motives and experiences can be derived.

According to the local Belfast newspaper, the *Irish News*, dated November 13th 1914, seventy members of the Irish National Volunteer Force had enlisted the day before at recruiting headquarters in Belfast. This was the same day and place that Robert and Michael Brennan had joined up. Michael had once stated that he was 'fighting for the freedom of Catholic Belgium and other small nations', the same motives that the Irish Volunteers under the guidance of Redmond had proclaimed. Seven days after enlisting, the brothers, together with friends and neighbours, attended Mass at St Patrick's chapel. They then assembled and marched through cheering Belfast crowds to the Great Northern Railway Station and the train to Fermoy, Co. Cork.

In 1915 after basic training the volunteers transferred to Aldershot in England. It was soon after this that the two brothers parted company. Robert was found to have a slight heart complaint and was transferred back to Ireland as part of the 4th Connaught Rangers. This was the unit that would provide provisions and back up services for the Connaught Rangers at the front line, and Robert was stationed at Bere Island, Co. Cork. Due to ill health he was discharged from the army in June 1916, but this was not the end of his fighting career, it was really only the beginning. This time, his enemy would be British, not German.

Robert Brennan joined the Irish Republican Army and was an Officer in Charge of C Company, Carrickhill Brigade, Belfast. He was never caught, arrested or interned for this involvement with the I.R.A. but indirectly, his wife Mary was. She spent time in Armagh Gaol, the women's prison. After a search of the family shop she was found to have two loaded revolvers hidden in her clothing, these belonged to two I.R.A. men who had sought refuge at the premises during a curfew in July

'Black and Tan' medal, awarded in 1966 to volunteers on the 50th anniversary of the Easter Rising

Robert Brennan and family

1922. Robert was reputedly on active service with Dan Breen in the Wicklow Mountains at the time of his wife's arrest and it was left to family and neighbours to look after the couple's young family. The youngest child, Robert Kevin, being so small, stayed with his mother in Armagh Gaol and took his first steps there. Robert Brennan died in 1973 and is buried near the Republican Plot in Milltown Cemetery.

Michael Brennan's war journey was a different one. He was allocated to the 6th Battalion of the Connaught Rangers and on 17th December 1915, along with 36 officers, 940 other men, 56 horses and mules, 4 machine guns, 17 vehicles and 10 bicycles, he set foot on French soil for the first time. His destination was eventually to be the front line trenches.

The first injury for the 6th Connaught Rangers happened on 15th January 1916 and the first deaths in the regiment occurred at the end of that same month, with four killed. But it was not German gunfire that would have a direct effect on Michael Brennan in these early days, it was the French weather. The War Diary for March 1916 tells that,

> the casualties during the period 1st–10th were 10 killed, 31 wounded and about 50 men sent to hospital suffering from exposure. Though our men were not severely tested under fire during this period they bore the extreme hardships of almost continuous fatigues through trenches in many places knee deep in mud and the long nights standing in that mud during cold wet and almost arctic weather with great fortitude and endurance.

Michael Brennan was more than likely one of these fifty men who suffered from exposure. It is known that about this time he was evacuated to a hospital in Dublin with gas poisoning and frostbite on his feet. It was whilst he was recuperating here that the 1916 Uprising took place and the ward in which he lay was taken over by the I.R.A. He was arrested by one of the rebel force whilst he lay ill and when asked many years later by his daughter Kathleen, 'What did you do daddy?' he replied, 'There was nothing I could do so I just lay in bed until it was all over.' Michael was later transferred back to Belfast to recuperate with his family and eventually he returned to France. He was promoted to Corporal.

On 21st March 1918 the 6th Connaught Rangers were caught up in the middle of the great German offensive and suffered heavy casualties. Charles A. Brett, a junior officer with the 6th and a native of Co. Antrim commented about this day many years later in his 'Recollections':

> Of the 650 odd men in the Battalion about 30 survived, mostly transport drivers and Battalion Headquarters staff, and even they had to fight hard. Most of the men were killed, very few were taken prisoner ... Happily Colonel Fielding survived, but the 6th Battalion as such ceased to exist.

Michael was one of these survivors. It is known that he saw his best friend killed and even though he was ordered to do so by a superior officer, he never shot a man who was trying to surrender. In later life Michael was traumatised by these events, suffering from what we now know as 'shellshock'. On one occasion whilst working at the family grocery shop he cut his hand with a knife, the sight of his own blood sent him into a panic frightening his children who witnessed the event. It was left to his wife Kitty to soothe him 'like a wee child' and to settle him.

On 13th April 1918 the 6th Connaught Rangers battalion was reduced to a training cadre and eventually it was amalgamated with the Leinster Regiment. Michael was transferred to the 2nd Leinsters and was discharged from service on 19th May 1919, two weeks before his 24th birthday.

But this was not the end of the story regarding Michael's involvement in the War. According to the official Medal Rolls of 1919 he was eligible for three medals, the 1915

Ministry of Home Affairs, Northern Ireland.

NO. *1345/342*.

MINUTE SHEET.

Mrs Mary Brennan.

Arrested 5: 6: 22.

D. I. Woods report. This woman
had two revolvers, one fully
loaded, hidden in her blouse.
There were two men in the house
at the time, *James O'Hara, *Wm
Morton, woman said the men
gave the revolvers to her & made
her hide them.

Detained in Armagh Prison, and
Reg 23. 7/6.

Prosecution ordered by A.G. under
Section 1. Fire Arms Act 1920. 21/6

Mary Brennan's arrest sheet

Star, the Victory Medal and the British War Medal. However, it is noted in these same documents that the Star was received back in the War Office in 1923, partial confirmation of the family story that Michael returned his medals. Whether these were returned directly on receipt in Belfast in protest at the War in general or as a reaction to the Belfast pogroms and the 1922 division of Ireland in particular, has not been ascertained. It is felt by some in the family that the latter reason would have been the deciding factor in any decision he had made. Michael and his wife had been the victims of the new Northern Ireland auxiliary police force, the 'B' Specials, who had ransacked their shop and home, robbing them. Also the aims for which Michael had striven when he initially joined the British Army in 1914 had proved futile. Ireland had not achieved Home Rule and was in fact partitioned. He was heard to say in later years that, 'there's nothing wrong with the British people, it is just their politicians that you can't trust.'

The medal that Michael Brennan took utmost pride in was the one he received as captain of Alton United football team of Carrickhill who won the F.A.I. Cup in 1923. This Belfast amateur side beat the foremost club in Ireland at that time, Shelbourne United, at a match at Dalymount Park on St Patrick's Day that year.

Michael died in 1979 and is buried in Milltown Cemetery, Belfast.

Brandhoek New Military Cemetery, Ieper (Ypres), Belgium. Source: www.cwgc.org

The Conlon Family

Cathal Donaghy

Owen Conlon, June 1915 (last photograph) prior to sailing on the *River Clyde* to Mudros, then from Mudros on *The Partridge* (5th Aug. 1915) to 'Watson's Pier', Anzac Cove on 6th Aug. then to Chunuk Bair

Had it not been for the sectarian riots of 1914 Owen and James Conlon may have finished their apprenticeships as mechanical engineers in Combe Barbour's Engineering Works. Like their father before them, Owen Conlon senior, they had worked in the Howard Street premises that ran between the nationalist Falls Road and the unionist Shankhill Road.

The sectarian hatred and tension of this time were politely glossed over in letter to Charles O'Hara, a relative of the Conlon family and a co-worker at Combe Barbour Ltd, when he applied for a reference from his former employers in 1938. The letter states that 'During the time he was with us we found him steady and attentive to his duties and he gave entire satisfaction. He left our employment through circumstances over which he had no control.'

Like many other working class Catholics at this time, finding any employment was difficult for the Conlons. Many families endured great hardship and deprivation and many breadwinners were forced to emigrate or join the British Army. The army attracted many of the 'laid off' Catholics because it offered them a wage to provide for their families. Enlistment was not based on loyalty to the crown, but survival.

Home Rule was promised to nationalists during

'We have loved him in life. let us not forget him in death."—St. Ambrose.

Sweet Heart of Jesus be Thou my love.—300 days.

Sweet Heart of Mary be my salvation.—300 days' indul.

O Sacred Heart of Jesus

HAVE MERCY ON THE SOUL OF

OWEN CONLON,

Killed at Dardanelles, on 10th August, 1915.

AGED 20 YEARS.

R.I.P

O Immense Passion! O Profound Wounds! O Profusion of Blood! O Sweetness above all Sweetness O Most Bitter Death! give him eternal rest —400 years' Indulgence.

Owen Conlon's memorial card

recruitment and many refused to join any of the six-county regiments preferring to enlist in an 'Irish' regiment. Owen Conlon senior joined the 6th Connaught Rangers in Galway, as did his sons, James and Owen junior. Owen senior and James (the latter promoted to sergeant) were sent to France. Owen senior returned home after the war, unharmed.

Owen junior was transferred to the Royal Irish Rifles and was sent to the Curragh Camp in Co. Kildare and after two weeks training he boarded a ship in Dublin bound for Southampton. After a further two days he boarded a troop ship called *The Partridge* which sailed to Mudros in Malta. On the 5th August 1915 *The Partridge* sailed toward the Gallipoli Peninsula where the R.I.R. disembarked by means of 'lighters' (small barges) at Watson's Pier, Anzac Cove. There they set up under bivouacs in Shrapnel Gully.

Owen Conlon junior, aged 20, became just another casualty on 10th August 1915 in the Battle of Sari Bair. For 259 days, from April 1915 to January 1916, 500,000 men were landed on Gallipoli, 300,000 of them became casualties, making Gallipoli yet another British fiasco in a war full of them.

Owen's mother Margaret tried to find news of her youngest son from the British Red

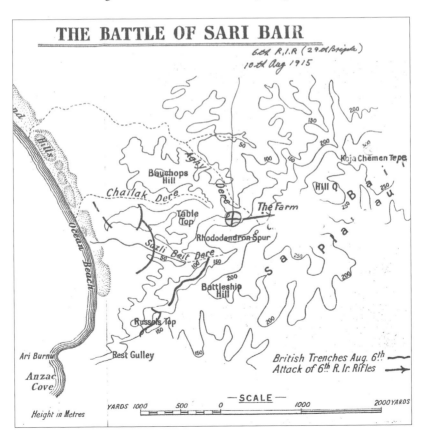

Combe Barbour workers: Sgt James Conlon
CR is front row, second from left

Cross Society in Dublin but to no avail. It was not until January 1917 that she was told that Rifleman Owen Conlon 10931 6th Bn, Royal Irish Rifles, was killed in action on 10th August 1915 in the Battle of Sari Bair, Gallipoli and that no remains were found. I discovered in 2002 that Owen Conlon is commemorated with honour on the Helles Memorial in Turkey.

Owen's death was difficult enough but there was then a double blow to my grandmother. In 1918 James Conlon of the 6th Connaught Rangers was wounded on the hand and after treatment in a French field hospital he returned to his unit but suffered mustard gas poisoning.

Sgt James Conlon, 2583, Connaught Rangers
Pte Owen Conlon, 10931, 6th Bn, Royal Irish
Rifles (seated). 1915

CONTRACTORS TO THE ADMIRALTY

Telegraphic Address
"COMBE, BELFAST."

CODES: BENTLEY'S, BENTLEY'S 2nd, A B C 5th AND 6th ED., A1, AND MARCONI INTERNATIONAL

Telephone
20814 (2 lines)

FAIRBAIRN LAWSON COMBE BARBOUR, LIMITED,

LEEDS AND BELFAST

ASSOCIATED WITH

URQUHART LINDSAY AND ROBERTSON ORCHAR LTD., DUNDEE.

BELFAST   12th August, 1938.

OUR REFERENCE......TB/AJ.........   YOUR REFERENCE....................

To whom it may concern

This is to certify that Charles O'Hara was employed
by us as an Apprentice Fitter from the 10/1/1917 to
the 20/7/1920.   During the time he was with us we
found him steady and attentive to his duties and he
gave entire satisfaction. He left our employment
through circumstances over which he had no control.

FAIRBAIRN LAWSON COMBE BARBOUR, Limited

Charles O'Hara's reference from Combe Barbour Ltd, Auugust 1938

He was discharged from the army on 15th May 1918 being 'No longer physically fit for War Service'. He died in Belfast two weeks later. James Conlon is buried in a family grave in Milltown Cemetery.

The Conlon brothers like many nationalist families went to war on a promise of Home Rule but when they returned they discovered that they had been deceived by the British Government. Many in the nationalist community have never accepted the rationale that forced family members into joining the British Army, while some unionists appear to have airbrushed from history the sacrifice made by those from nationalist areas who fought and died in this war. Ninety-plus years later they are remembered with honour and pride by their families and many others.

Tommy 'Topper' Devlin

Bobby Devlin

My father Tommy 'Topper' Devlin was a Connaught Ranger during the Great War. He fought on the Somme in 1916 and was wounded twice. He also did stints in the Pioneer Corps and the Royal Irish Fusiliers.

He was one of the many Irish Volunteers duped into joining the British Army on a promise that Ireland would achieve Home Rule. They were urged to do this by the Irish Parliamentary Party leaders John Redmond and Joe Devlin.

Being a Falls Road man he, like many returning soldiers, joined the Irish Republican Army and served through the War for Irish Independence.

At the turn of the century my father was chased out of Harland and Wolff in Belfast where he had worked as a fitter. Like many other Catholics he ended up in Glasgow where he found employment in John Brown's shipyard. It was in Glasgow that he found his great love. No, not my mother, it was Glasgow Celtic! In 1914 when the bugle sounded he returned to Belfast joining the Irish Volunteers.

Topper was born at 59 Balmer Street in 1891. The family moved to 46 Lady Street. In 1924 he married Annie Lillis of 32 Conway Street. Her father was a career soldier, Sergeant-Major Patrick Lillis who served in the Great War

Tommy 'Topper' Devlin

with the Royal Enniskillen Fusiliers. Dad had an older brother, my Uncle Johnny who was in the Indian Army and died during the Great flu epidemic at the end of the war.

After a sojourn in Beechmount Parade the Devlin finally settled at 80 Conway Street. My parents' last abode was Rossnaree right on the Shaws Road.

Just before he died in 1977 I used to sit and yarn with him about that period 1914–1922. I remember asking him about the Raglan Street ambush. He laughed aloud when he described the claims of so many men who took part in this event, which had gone down in Falls Road history. If that had been the case then it would have been worse that 'Custer's Last Stand.'

I have a treasury of memories about my Da, Topper Devlin. A tough, lovable wee man of great integrity. I can still see him there on his favourite chair with his hearing aid at the ready. The only time he switched it off was when Annie Devlin starting giving off.

His wee grin is forever in my thoughts.

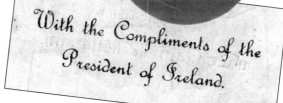

With the Compliments of the President of Ireland.

Pte Patrick Donelly (left), 6th Connaught Rangers, with two comrades in Cairo, Egypt, post-war

Patrick Donnelly

Harry Donaghy

Patrick Donnelly was born on the 21st of March 1892 at number 10 Inkerman Street just off the Falls Road. He left school at 12 years of age to begin work in Grieves' Mill. In his early teens he then went to work with his father, Joseph, in the building trade. Paddy was an ardent supporter of the Irish Parliamentary Party and its local M.P. Joe Devlin. In 1912 he joined the Irish National Volunteers, and along with thousands of others, he attended the rallies and meetings organised by the I.P.P. in support of Home Rule.

In the summer of 1914 as the prospect of War in Europe was becoming ever more real he heard the call from John Redmond and the leadership of the I.P.P. that the Volunteers should enlist in the British Army as a means of achieving Home Rule for

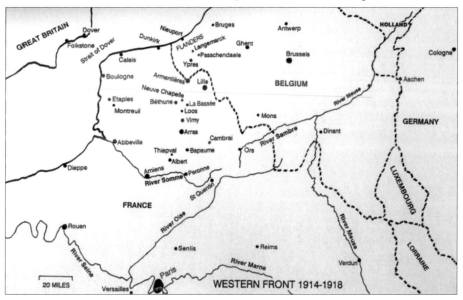

WESTERN FRONT 1914-1918

Ireland. When War was finally declared, on the 4th August 1914, Paddy, along with hundreds of others from that part of Belfast, enlisted with the Connaught Rangers at the R.I.C. Barracks in Divis Street, which was one of many recruiting stations across Belfast.

His younger brother Tom enlisted at the same time, and almost a year later on the 7th August 1915, Tom was killed in action at Gallipoli serving with the Royal Irish

Fusiliers. During the course of the War Paddy saw action on the Western Front, Mesopotamia and Palestine and was wounded on two occasions during his service.

Paddy could be called one of the lucky ones. He survived while many of those he knew and were dear to him did not. As a result of his War service when he was demobbed in 1919 he got a job as a stoker in Belfast Gas Works. He was one of the very few Catholics to be employed in what was believed to be one of the many deeply sectarianised industries of the time.

Like many of those who had survived and returned home he spoke only rarely about his experiences. He did refer on occasions to his brother Tom whose grave was so far away on the shores of the Dardanelles and regretted that no one from the family would be able to visit. He also spoke with fondness about the two brothers of his wife, Elizabeth, both of whom he knew well before the War. Johnny and Dominic Adams, from Varna Street, were killed within a week of each other in May 1915 on the Western Front. Johnny was serving with the 1st Battalion of the Royal Irish Rifles and Dominic was serving with the 2nd Battalion, Royal Inniskilling Fusiliers.

Paddy Donnelly's story is probably a fair reflection of many other stories of men from that generation and time. It is only recently that opportunities to tell some of these stories have become possible for those who came after them. Many wish to look again with compassion and understanding at the realities and circumstances that their forebears lived in and experienced.

Postcard sent home by a 6th Connaught Ranger showing a memorial to the Battle of Fontenoy. It reads: 'In memory of the heroic Irish soldiers who changed defeat into victory at Fontenoy, 11 May 1745'. The French victory was the result of the celebrated charge of their Irish Brigade. They turned an imminent defeat into victory but lost 750 killed and wounded. The Connaughts fought as 'The Scotch Brigade' on the British side at Fontenoy

Patrick McKillen

Robin McKillen

EARLY LIFE

Patrick McKillen was born in 1885 in 27 Malcolmson Street, Springfield Road, Belfast. He was the fifth of six children who all attended St Paul's primary school in nearby Cavendish Street. In 1899 Patrick's parents, John and Catherine McKillen, moved with their young family to 60 Oranmore Street, Springfield Road, where Patrick grew up enjoying a very happy childhood. In his youth he was a keen cyclist in Clonard cycling club and was an avid whist player. His brother John was also a keen cyclist but because he had an infant son and his wife was expecting their second child he was the only member of Clonard cycling club who did not enlist in the British Army at the outbreak of World War One.

Prior to enlistment in 1914 Patrick was employed as fireman in the firm of Messrs Wm Ross and Co., Clonard Mills, Belfast. (Known locally as Ross's Mill). He became engaged to Mary C. McCann of Dunmore Street. Mary Catherine was the eldest child of John Joseph McCann, a machine master, and Catherine McCann who lived at number 49. Dunmore Street ran back to back with Oranmore Street. They would have known each other since childhood.

The house with the glass door in two halves is 60 Oranmore Street. Apart from the new front door the house is unchanged since 1898 when John Snr and his wife Catherine occupied it as a new house. In September 1914 Patrick walked out through the door and turned to his left to walk to the tram stop on the nearby Springfield Road. Mary McCann walked with him 'to see him off.' As was the custom of the time she would have linked her right arm through his left arm as they walked.

John senior and his wife Catherine stood in the doorway and watched their son go off to war in Flanders Fields. Their hearts were heavy with foreboding

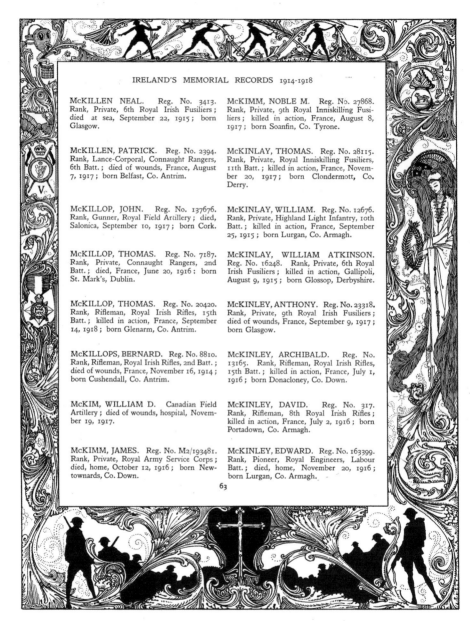

McKILLEN NEAL. Reg. No. 3413. Rank, Private, 6th Royal Irish Fusiliers; died at sea, September 22, 1915; born Glasgow.

McKILLEN, PATRICK. Reg. No. 2394. Rank, Lance-Corporal, Connaught Rangers, 6th Batt.; died of wounds, France, August 7, 1917; born Belfast, Co. Antrim.

McKILLOP, JOHN. Reg. No. 137676. Rank, Gunner, Royal Field Artillery; died, Salonica, September 10, 1917; born Cork.

McKILLOP, THOMAS. Reg. No. 7187. Rank, Private, Connaught Rangers, 2nd Batt.; died, France, June 20, 1916: born St. Mark's, Dublin.

McKILLOP, THOMAS. Reg. No. 20420. Rank, Rifleman, Royal Irish Rifles, 15th Batt.; killed in action, France, September 14, 1918; born Glenarm, Co. Antrim.

McKILLOPS, BERNARD. Reg. No. 8810. Rank, Rifleman, Royal Irish Rifles, 2nd Batt.; died of wounds, France, November 16, 1914; born Cushendall, Co. Antrim.

McKIM, WILLIAM D. Canadian Field Artillery; died of wounds, hospital, November 19, 1917.

McKIMM, JAMES. Reg. No. M2/193481. Rank, Private, Royal Army Service Corps; died, home, October 12, 1916; born Newtownards, Co. Down.

McKIMM, NOBLE M. Reg. No. 27868. Rank, Private, 9th Royal Inniskilling Fusiliers; killed in action, France, August 8, 1917; born Soanfin, Co. Tyrone.

McKINLAY, THOMAS. Reg. No. 28115. Rank, Private, Royal Inniskilling Fusiliers, 11th Batt.; killed in action, France, November 20, 1917; born Clondermott, Co. Derry.

McKINLAY, WILLIAM. Reg. No. 12676. Rank, Private, Highland Light Infantry, 10th Batt.; killed in action, France, September 25, 1915; born Lurgan, Co. Armagh.

McKINLAY, WILLIAM ATKINSON. Reg. No. 16248. Rank, Private, 6th Royal Irish Fusiliers; killed in action, Gallipoli, August 9, 1915; born Glossop, Derbyshire.

McKINLEY, ANTHONY. Reg. No. 23318. Rank, Private, 9th Royal Irish Fusiliers; died of wounds, France, September 9, 1917; born Glasgow.

McKINLEY, ARCHIBALD. Reg. No. 13165. Rank, Rifleman, Royal Irish Rifles, 15th Batt.; killed in action, France, July 1, 1916; born Donacloney, Co. Down.

McKINLEY, DAVID. Reg. No. 317. Rank, Rifleman, 8th Royal Irish Rifles; killed in action, France, July 2, 1916; born Portadown, Co. Armagh.

McKINLEY, EDWARD. Reg. No. 163399. Rank, Pioneer, Royal Engineers, Labour Batt.; died, home, November 20, 1916; born Lurgan, Co. Armagh.

Entry for Patrick McKillen from *Ireland's Memorial Records 1914–1918*

WAR SERVICE

Patrick enlisted in the 6th Battalion of the Connaught Rangers Regiment which had been formed at Kilworth camp on 14th September 1914 under Army Order 382 (1914). When the 5th (Service) Battalion moved to Dublin the 6th moved to Fermoy. Patrick's regimental number was 2394. He served in D company.

Patrick McKillen

Before leaving Belfast Patrick made a pact with his brother John, who was married at this time with a young son, (Sean), that he (Patrick) would join the army first and if it proved agreeable then he would 'send for John' and possibly their father. The family had at this time an old dog called Jack. Later when conditions in the trenches had become appallingly bad Patrick wrote to John warning him not to enlist. I would not let 'old Jack' come out here, he wrote.

After their arrival in the trenches in early 1916 the 6th saw action in trench raiding parties and in supporting several English regiments who were under great pressure. Later, in preparation for the forthcoming battles which were to become known as the Battle of the Somme, all soldiers were required to make out a will. The wills are now in the National Archives, Dublin.

In late July 1916 the 6th saw extensive action in the Puits 14 bis sector where they took many casualties. Patrick was awarded a certificate of gallantry.

SINGLE HANDED

Belfast INV man who held position 24hrs with machine gun.

Private Patrick McKillen, machine gun section, Connaught Rangers, whose parents reside at 60 Oranmore Street Belfast, has been presented with a parchment certificate signed by Major General W B. Hickie, Commanding 16th Irish Division, which reads as follows: – 'I have read with much pleasure the reports of your Regimental Commander and Brigade Commander regarding your gallant conduct and devotion to duty in the field on July 27th 1916, and have ordered your name and deed to be entered in the records of the Irish Division.'

The Commanding Officer of the Battalion, in a letter, says that private McKillen continued to work his machine gun single handed, under a heavy fire. After all the remainder of the section had been put out of action private McKillen stuck to his gun and held the position for 24 hrs. He was a member of D company. Belfast regiment. Irish National Volunteers.

Irish News, Saturday, 19 July 1919

The 6th were involved in many actions during the summer of 1916 the most famous being the battle for the French village of Guillemont.

INFORMAL WILL.

W.O. No.: E/ *403353/1.*

DOMICILE, *Irish*

Record No. *253/457476*

1/18. The enclosed document

dated *1st April 1916*

Name *Patrick McKillen* and signed

Patrick McKillen.

Regtl. No. *6/2394 L/Cpl*
and Rank

appears to have been written

or executed by the person

Regt. *6th Bn Connaught* named in the margin while
Rangers.

he was "in actual military

service" within the meaning

Died at *in France* of the Wills Act, 1837, and

has been recognised by the

Date of Death *7/8/1)* War Department as con-

stituting a valid will.

WAR OFFICE.

for the Assistant Financial Secretary.

Date *22nd February 1918*

H. 15/1905.

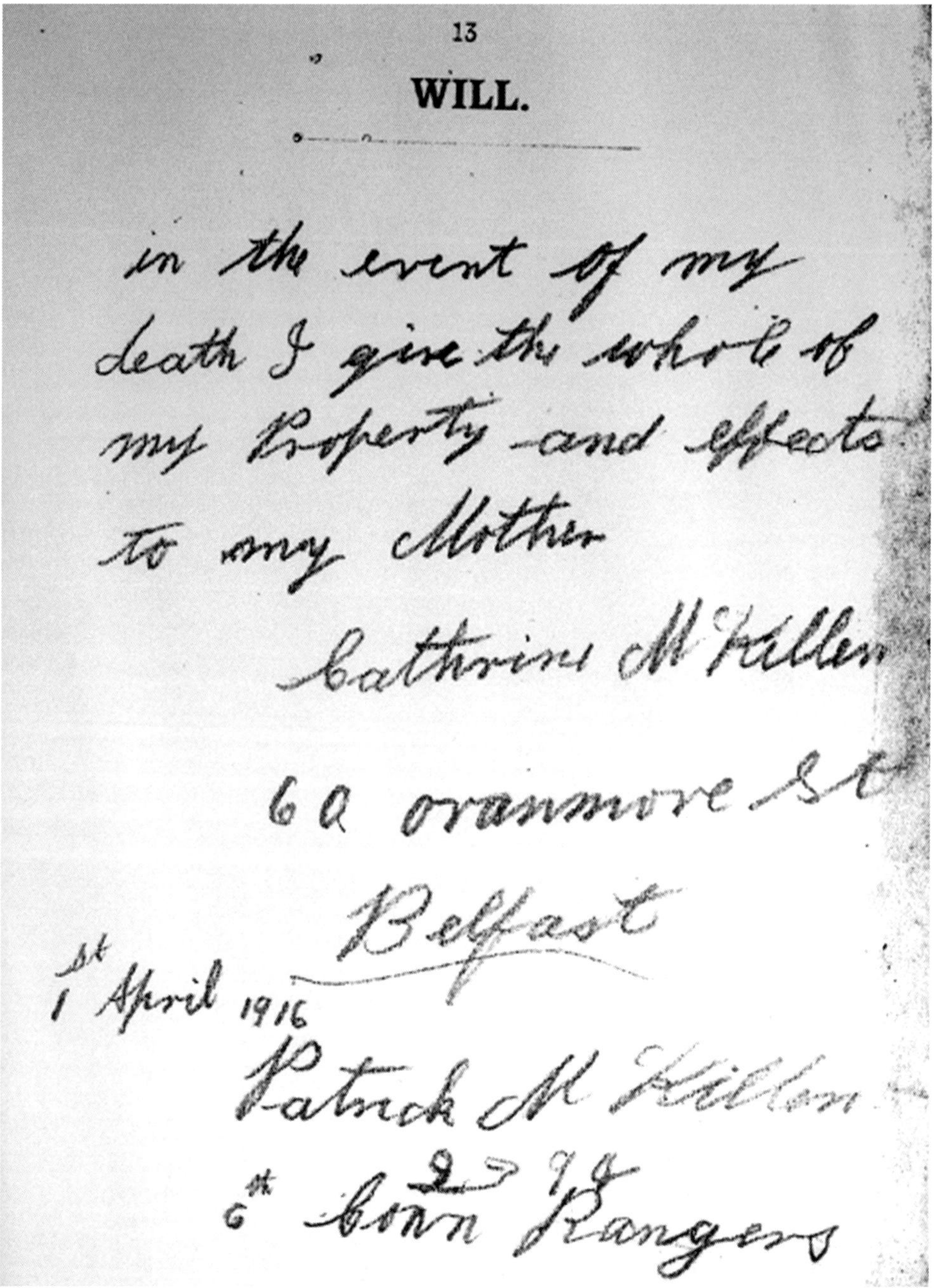

WILL.

in the event of my
death I give the whole of
my Property and effects
to my Mother

Cathrine Mc Killen

6 a oranmore St

Belfast

1st April 1916

Patrick Mc Killen

6th Conn Rangers

Patrick's will made out on 1st April 1916

THE BATTLE FOR GUILLEMONT

On September 3rd 1916 the 6th went into action at Guillemont. This was one of the great and costly battles of the Somme. Patrick and his fellow soldiers performed heroic feats of gallantry in the face of very heavy enemy fire.

> The charge of the IRISH TROOPS through GUILLEMONT on Sept 3rd was one of the most astonishing feats of the war … They stormed the first, second, third German lines, sweeping all resistance away. They were men uplifted, out of themselves, 'fey' as the Scots would call it. The whole attack from first to last was a model of efficiency, organisation, and courage. All the qualities that go to the making of victory were there, fitting in with each other, balancing each other, making a terrific weapon driven by a high spirit. The artillery was in perfect union with the infantry – the most difficult thing in war. The brigadiers & the officers carried out the general plan to the letter; & the men! – It is impossible to over praise the men, who were wonderful in courage, and wonderful in discipline.
>
> So GUILLEMONT was taken and held, not only by great gunfire, but by men inspired with some spirit beyond their ordinary courage. And one day these troops will carry the name upon their colours, so that the World may remember.
>
> PHILIP GIBB – *Battles of the Somme*

> The troops taking part in the attack on Guillemont were the 7th Brigade (Irish) including the following regiments –
> 6th Connaught Rangers,
> 6th Royal Irish
> 7th Leinsters,
> and the 8th Munsters.
> The attack was led by the 6th Connaught Rangers commanded by Col. J.S.M. Lenox-Conyngham.

Even after taking such heavy casualties and the loss of both Colonel and second-in-command there was no rest for the Connaught Rangers. On the 6th of September Major Rowland Fielding D.S.O. was given temporary command of the 6th and joined the remnants of the Battalion on a slope alongside the ruins of Carnoy in preparation for an attack on the village of Ginchy. Of the 250 Connaught Rangers remaining for battle only 109 were from the original draft of 952 in 1914. There were further heavy casualties at Ginchy.

Major Fielding writes,

> September 9th. Trenches, facing Ginchy … The right battalion moved forward at 4.45, having presumably failed to hear of the postponement … I cannot say whether this caused our artillery to abandon the last two minutes of 'intensive bombardment' … When the 47th Brigade left the trench at 4.47 it was immediately mowed down as it crossed the parapet.

The Connaught Rangers were withdrawn for a long period of rest and refurbishment after this action. For the next eleven months they were engaged in a series of skirmishes and trench raiding parties in strength which ended with the Battle of Messines (Mesen).

On August 2nd 1917 the Connaught Rangers were withdrawn from the Messines (Mesen) area and, in a temporary transfer to the 15th Division, were sent, via Ypres (Ieper) and the Menin Gate to the old British front system on the right sector of the Corps front. They relieved the 6th Bn, Royal Irish Regiment. A, B and C companies were on the reverse slope of Frezenberg Ridge while D company was on the forward slope in full view of the enemy. Two enemy aircraft flew low over the front lines and were followed by heavy and accurate shelling at noon. The rain was so heavy and mud so bad that the Lewis guns and rifles would not fire. It was about this stage that enemy grenades were thrown into Patrick's trench and he was injured. Family oral tradition says he died of his wounds the next day but he died on the 7th and on the 6th the Battalion had been rested. It is more likely that he was injured on the 5th August and died on the 7th. It was also common practice for the Army to spare the family as much pain as possible and the worst dismemberment would have been reported as 'died of his wounds', 'a bullet through the heart', we shall never know.

The Battlefields at Ypres saw the greatest carnage of the entire war. One in three men who died in World War One died at Ypres.

Mary C. McCann never married. She grieved for Patrick all her long life.

Patrick McKillen's Medal Card (WO 372/13, The National Archives, Kew)

Flowers are laid on Patrick's grave in Brandhoek New Military Cemetery, (Ieper) on 17th May 2006. They are in the regimental colours of green and yellow

BIBLIOGRAPHY

Guillemont, Somme, Michael Stedman, Leo Cooper, Pen & Sword Books, 1998.
The Fierce Light, Anne Powell, Sutton Publishing Limited, 2006.
The German Army at Passchendaele, Jack Sheldon, Pen & Sword Books, 2007.
Tracing British Battalions on the Somme, Ray Westlake, Pen & Sword Books, 2009.
The Battles of the Somme, Philip Gibbs, McClelland, Goodchild and Stewart Publishers, 1917, several reprints.

James Patrick McKenna

Jonathan Savage

My great grandfather James Patrick McKenna was born on the 25th July 1888, the son of John McKenna, Managing Director of McKenna & McGinley Aerated Water of Bath Place, Belfast (near Divis Street). James was the fourth of five children born to John and his wife Mary and at the time of his birth the family were living at 65 Nail Street. The McKennas would later live at 25 Raglan Street and 287 Falls Road, near to where the Beechmount Leisure Centre would be sited today.

My curiosity in James McKenna was awakened after finding 40 postcards that had been sent by him from the front lines in France to his wife back in Belfast. These postcards were not only of a personal nature but were a primary source material with which I could put together a picture of James' time and experiences of the First World War. Today, with the story of the Connaught Rangers and the involvement of those men from the Falls Road and West Belfast area who fought in WW1 fast approaching 100 years, it is vitally important that their story is told and remembered.

James Patrick McKenna married Mary (Minnie) Gallagher on 12th April 1910, four years before any hint of war. Mary, from Iris Street, was supported on her big day by her sister Jane and Jane's future husband John Bernard Stuart. They too would experience the worst that war could bring. John Stuart would die of wounds received at Le Cateau, France on 18th October 1918 just weeks away from the eventual end of

James Patrick McKenna, second from the left, with colleagues
from Hughes Dickson Flour Mill, Belfast

hostilities. John Bernard Stuart had served with the 2nd Battalion of the Royal Dublin Fusiliers.

This was not the only tragedy to befall the Gallagher sisters as Minnie and Jane also had a half sister, Sarah, who was born in 1876. Sarah too would marry a man who would later enlist for the war with tragic circumstances. Her husband Private Bernard Kerr (20949) of the 9th Battalion, Royal Irish Fusiliers, would be killed in action on 12th April 1918; he is remembered on the Tyne Cot Memorial in Belgium.

Like many men from the Falls Road area, James Patrick McKenna enlisted in the 6th Battalion of the Connaught Rangers. Information about his enlistment is scant, however as James was a proud Irishman and a Gaelic speaker, I believe it would be directly related to the influence of Joe Devlin and the anticipation of Home Rule for Ireland.

After enlistment James McKenna along with the other Belfast men departed from the Great Northern Railway Station to cheering Belfast crowds. They then travelled on to Fermoy, Co. Cork to undergo basic training and on completion of this they were later shipped as part of the 16th Irish Division to Aldershot, England. A postcard sent by James McKenna from Aldershot in 1915 states, ' ... there is only about 300 men with us at present so we will need another 900 men before going to France ... most of the chaps are away unfit ...'. To me this highlights the eagerness of men to volunteer for the 16th Irish Division, they did so despite being in various states of poor health.

James McKenna, now Corporal McKenna (4370) was allocated to serve as a Machine Gunner in the 6th Connaught Rangers. The Regiment left England for Le Havre with 36 Officers and 952 other ranks and arrived at Hesdigneul near Béthune on the 19th December 1915. After training and work with the trench parties the Connaught Rangers moved to the front on 26th January 1916. Just before this deployment to the front James sent a postcard home (20th January 1916) and on it he stated how he had fared over the previous Christmas away from home, '... I have got more cigs chocolate and tobacco also Christmas puddings this while back that my belly is sore eating'. Clearly spirits were high before moving to the trenches on the 26th as there were

An idealised image of 'the girl I left behind'. The inference is that she is waiting for her 'hero' who will return home safely

no fears being transmitted home, nor was there any indication as to the later brutalities of the Somme that the Connaught Rangers would experience.

The story of the 6th Battalion Connaught Rangers is an important chapter in Irish nationalist history and the men who fought in the trenches of World War One did so because they believed it would gain favour for Ireland in respect of Home Rule. Not all nationalists thought this way however and on Easter Sunday 1916 at the GPO in Dublin events took place which would later change the politics of the country and eventually contribute to the separation of a nation. Whatever knowledge or sentiments that James and his colleagues at the front felt about the Rising back in Ireland, no indication was sent home in his postcard of 26th April 1916, which states

> ... I hope you enjoyed Easter Holidays we had good weather and a good time but the Germans kept on shelling us especially on Easter Sunday the big shell dropped close to the chapel but did not strike it.

So while the Germans shelled the Irish in France the British also shelled the Irish in Dublin. It is unknown when James and his fellow soldiers became aware of the events back in Ireland or of their attitudes towards what was unfolding. Perhaps James knew that any favourable comments about the Rising in his correspondence would not have passed the censors' scrutiny. But it is more likely that he and his comrades were more concerned with the situation that they found themselves in or at the time did not think the Rising was significant enough to comment on.

In July 1916 James McKenna fought at the Somme. He was injured in the face by shrapnel from a German shell and was hospitalised. On his return to the front he wrote home to Belfast, his words this time, were concerned with hearing from home and also indicating, perhaps because of his near miss with a German shell, some fear for his future,

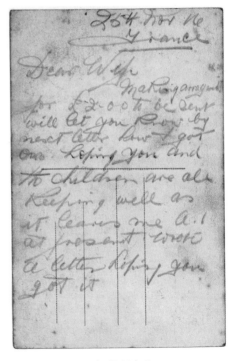

> ... I hope to hear from you soon, I thought you would have answered my letters to hear how I was as I was out of the hospital last Tuesday. Well things are very hot at present

For many joining the British Army was a way to support their families. Even though James McKenna was fighting on the front line he was still making arrangements to send money home to his family in Belfast

here ... I am expecting a big battle to come off soon just on our left there is a big battle on at present so perhaps it will extend to us. If you can I would like you would send *Thompson Weekly* – remaining your loving husband Jim.

Unfortunately, quite a few of the postcards sent home to Belfast were undated with the result being that some of the places and events that James experienced cannot be put into proper context. However, despite messages being very short, we can get a glimpse into army life and how important contact with home was to the soldiers and how those back at home were glad of any news, to know their loved ones were still alive: 'I am 3 days on the march to some new front I cannot say where I am where I am going. Anyway I am quite well. Jim'.

Thankfully James survived the battles and challenges that came his way whilst serving with the Connaught Rangers. He remained in the army until 1919 and a postcard dated 18th February that year showed that he was still kept occupied even though the war had been over for several months. This time his work, whatever that had entailed, was with 126 POW Company.

'Dear wife, [I] received your kind and ever welcome letter, glad to see you and the children are keeping well. I will write a letter later on as I am busy at present. Jim'

On his return to Belfast my great grandfather got employment as a cart loader, shipping bags of flour, at Hughes Dickson Flour Mill in Belfast. He went on to have 8 children with his wife Minnie and lived at number 50 Forest Street (beside Mackies). He died in July 1954 and is buried in Milltown Cemetery.

I have since found out that there were hundreds of these postcards sent home by my great grandfather during the War and from the message sent home in one card it seems it was always his intention to treasure these mementos.

' Dear wife, I am try [sic] to send a box which I got with chocolate in to keep these as I want to frame them with feet work if I come home again ...'.

Placed onto a table as he had intended to do, and covered with glass, these postcards remained in the family home. However over the years many were lost and some were sold in Smithfield Market. The lost postcards may still be in circulation today and are most likely owned by memorabilia collectors. The few that remain within the family give an invaluable reminder into this period of James' life and of the sacrifices made by so many Belfast men during the First World War.

Patrick O'Hare

Seán O'Hare

My grandfather Patrick O'Hare was born on the 4th of May 1883 in Ormond Street, Belfast to Michael and Maggie O'Hare who came originally from the Kilcoo area of County Down.

Patrick married my grandmother, Margaret Brankin from nearby McDonnell Street around the year 1900, the beginning of the new century. Paddy's first job as a coach painter and sign writer was cut short when he had a severe reaction to the chemicals used in the paint at that time. Out of a job, he joined the British Army in 1904 and served as a sergeant up until the disbandment of the Connaughts in 1922. Patrick was not the only member of his family to join the army, his only bother Ned joined the 6th Connaught Rangers in 1914; he was invalided out in December 1916. Two of Margaret's brothers were also to serve during World War One.

Perhaps as a result of the Mutiny in India in 1920, the memory of the 6th Connaughts is unique for a British Army regiment in West Belfast, it was held with some regard. For instance, the story is told how in St Peter's bingo hall the number 88 was called, not as two fat ladies, but as '88 Connaught Rangers' (their regimental number) and a cheer would be heard from the locals in the hall. It was through the investigation of this phenomenon, and family histories that led to the formation of the Sixth Connaught Rangers Research Group.

The story of the Urney Street horror which took place in 1921 and which is transcribed below (from a report which appeared in the *Irish News* at the time) left an indelible mark on the O'Hare family and influenced the descendants of Paddy.

Irish News and Belfast Morning News
Tuesday, 21st June 1921

THE EVICTIONS

CONNAUGHT RANGER'S PLIGHT

Many cases of savage cruelty could be cited; but possibly the limit in terrorism was reached in the case of a man who currently wears the King's uniform – and has worn it for the past sixteen years. The victim in this case was P O'Hare, whose wife and family of small children lived in Urney Street. He has served in the Connaught Rangers for the past sixteen years and with distinction in the Great War. Last week he was home on furlough – and what a week of furlough it was. A reign of terror set up around his little home, his wife and children constantly in a state of panic and alarm, hoping against hope that their turn for eviction would not come. But their hopes were vain. On one of the nights that the Orange mobs were particularly active one section, armed with revolvers, numbering over a hundred, rushed down Urney Street and commenced to smash the windows and doors of O'Hare's home. They got into the house and proceeded to smash the furniture in the kitchen. O'Hare, who was in uniform at the time, had his wife and children upstairs. Not content with smashing the furniture, the gang of rowdies went one better in cruelty and terrorism. They surrounded O'Hare and his family, dragged them downstairs, and then told Mrs O'Hare that they were going to shoot her husband. One would have thought that O'Hare's uniform would have saved him and his home, but no – he was a Catholic; that was a sufficient crime. His wife and children were pushed out into the street, and he was dragged into the yard. Mrs. O'Hare began to scream in the street, naturally thinking that she would see her husband alive no more. Suddenly a shot rang out, and this confirmed her worst fears. Fortunately, the attackers did not carry out their threat. After some time they allowed him to leave the house – not to go back again – but could one imagine a more dastardly piece of fiendish cruelty and terrorism? O'Hare returned to England last night, leaving behind his family without a hearth or home to call their own. They are now living in the premises already referred to in which some fifty refugees are housed.

Several cases of a similar nature occurred, but the fact that O'Hare was wearing the King's uniform shows in a brilliant light the attitude and mentality of the Orange gangs of gunmen.

This family history and the re-telling of harrowing stories to us as children growing up influenced our outlook in later years. We preferred to concentrate on the republican dimension of our country's history, choosing to ignore Paddy and his time with the Connaughts outside of the home. This attitude has now changed and I now hold my grandfather's activities with the same respect as all those who fought for the betterment of the people of this island. Thankfully, this maturing of attitudes is spreading and I hope the telling of our family story will play a part in highlighting the commonalties between us in our divided communities.

My Grandmother and her children spent some time living in the abandoned pub mentioned above, which was on the corner of Craig Street and Falls Road. Later, Paddy secured army accommodation in London for his wife and the younger children; the family remained there until after the end of his service. Patrick O'Hare's War medals were returned unclaimed.

By the time he returned to Belfast two of Paddy's elder sons were members of the I.R.A. – one a Belfast delegate to the I.R.A. army convention in Dublin in 1922. Most of his nine children were to become active republicans, a conviction carried down to the present. By the outbreak of the Second World War, one of his sons, two of his daughters and a grandson were in prison for Republican activity.

How much the Urney Street tragedy influenced the politics of the family, which followed the general political trend throughout Ireland, is impossible to judge from this distant standpoint. Just to say that growing up I heard more than my share of anti-British and anti-Unionist politicking, but there was little anti-Protestant rhetoric.

After the family's return from England they were housed in Amcomri Street, in a house built with funds raised by Irish Americans for refugees of the troubles. Paddy got a job with the *Irish News* where he worked until his death in 1934 aged 52 years. He took no active part in politics.

Sergeant Paddy O'Hare (right) pictured with Billy
Wilkie (left), a Protestant war veteran from the
Falls Road, taken outside the Bee Hive Bar, *c.* 1930

The 6th Connaught Rangers Timeline

Robin McKillen

On the 20th November 1914 the Connaught Ranger volunteers left Belfast's Great Victoria Street station and after a short stop in Dublin proceeded to Fermoy, County Cork. They were billeted in the New Barracks where they commenced their basic army training with visits to the nearby Kilworth camp for rifle practice. At Kilworth they were also trained in trench construction, trench raiding parties and in the operation of the trench mortar.

Fermoy railway station 2010. It is unchanged since the Connaught Rangers arrived here in 1914. They exited the station through its main entrance and were met by members of Fermoy Irish National Volunteers. Accompanied by the Cross Street National Band, the Barrack Hill Band and the Pipers' Band they marched to the New Barracks

In November 1914 the 6th Connaught Rangers became a unit of the 47th (Irish) Brigade. The 47th Brigade then comprised the 6th CR, 6th Battalion the Royal Irish Rifles, 7th Battalion the Leinster Regiment and the 8th Battalion the Royal Munster Fusiliers.

In February 1915 the 47th Brigade concentrated at Kilworth camp where it trained until August, it then became part of the 16th Irish Division. The 6th Connaught Rangers were then entrained to Blackdown Camp in Aldershot. They had a stop over and day off in Dublin to allow the men to attend Mass on the 15th of August for the feast of the Assumption of Our Blessed Lady. Many of them took advantage of a day in Dublin to have their photographs taken in uniform to send home as a postcard to their families in Belfast. The preferred photographer was T. Kirg, 5 North Earl St., Dublin (Under the Clock).

There was some delay between the recruitment of the 6th Connaught Rangers and the battalion's movement to France as part of the 47th Brigade. This was due to the constant siphoning-off of experienced soldiers to fill the casualty gaps in other frontline regiments already in France. In particular they lost many units to the Guards Division. However, by the end of November 1915 the 6th Battalion the Connaught Rangers was in a state of readiness.

On 17th December, under the command of Lieutenant-Colonel J.S.M. Lenox-Conyngham, the 6th proceeded by rail, via Farnborough, to Southampton for embarkation to Le Havre. On arrival at Le Havre on the 18th the strength of the 6th was 36 officers and 952 other ranks. That night they left for Hesdigneul near Béthune and arrived on the 19th. After training and trench parties around Hesdigneul the battalion moved up to the trenches on 26th January 1916. They were positioned to the left of Loos in the Puits 14 bis sector and were now attached to the 46th Infantry Brigade.

February 29th 1916 – Moved to Annequin Fosse attached to the 36th Infantry Brigade.

March 31st 1916 – Moved to rest in billets at Noeux-Les-Mines.

April 1st 1916 – Soldiers in the 6th Connaught Rangers were required to make out their Wills.

August 13th 1916 – Meculte.

September 3rd 1916 – The 6th went into action at Guillemont. This was one of the great and costly battles of the Somme in which the 6th CR performed many heroic feats of gallantry in the face of very heavy enemy fire. They achieved much but Lieutenant-Colonel Lenox-Conyngham was killed in action while bravely leading his men forward in an inspiring charge.

Our commander stepped out and pointed to the Position with his cane 'that, Connaught Rangers, Is what you have got to take' was all he said.

His wooden grave cross was sent home (after a permanent memorial was erected) and was placed below a wall tablet in Armagh Church of Ireland Cathedral where it stands today. The inscription reads:

These crosses were first erected
At Carnoy on the Somme
By the Officers and Men of the 6th Connaught Rangers
In the 16th Irish Division
Over the grave of their commanding officer
Lt Col. J.S.M. Lenox-Conyngham
After a lifetime of service with the regiment
At the age of 54 on September 3rd 1916
Fell leading his battalion

To the capture of Guillemont.
O DEATH WHERE IS THY STING

Go through the Cathedral's main entrance and walk
up the right side aisle. At the end of this aisle go
through the large wrought iron gates and into the
military chapel. Immediately through the gates of
the chapel look left. The wooden grave cross is fixed
to the wall below the bronze tablet. The original
6th battalion colours are still attached

Major R.C. Fielding of the special reserve of the Coldstream Guards was given
temporary command of the 6th. He wrote a series of frequent letters home to his wife
in England and these contain a wealth of information on the movement and actions of
the 6th Bn. He writes,

> September 10th. Happy Valley. It is over. The men were in no condition for
> battle of this strenuous order, as I had thought before. Those that were not raw
> recruits from the new drafts were worn out and exhausted by their recent
> fighting, and much more fitted for a rest camp than an attack. During the three
> days my casualties have amounted to 9 officers and 83 other ranks out of the 16
> officers and 250 other ranks with which I started. The total casualties of the 6th
> Battalion for the last nine days have been 23 officers and 407 other ranks.
>
> Anne Powell (Quoted from *The Fierce Light*)

September 12th 1916 – The 6th was sent to Vaux-Sur-Somme for rest until the 18th.

September 18th 1916 – Left Vaux-Sur-Somme and marched to Corbie where they were taken by bus to Huppy Till.

September 21st 1916 – Marched to Abbyville and then entrained to Bailleul when they were marched again to Metern and finally to billets at Fontaine Houck.

September 24th 1916 – To St Jean Cappel and then to Locre (Loker).

September 27th 1916 – Moved to the trenches in the Vierstraat sector.

October 29th 1916 – The battalion saw fierce action before Grand Bois and sustained heavy casualties. Patrick McKillen lost many friends and neighbours in these actions at Grand Bois.

November 5th 1916 – Relieved to 'Curragh' camp, Locre (Loker) until the 14th. Then back to the trenches.

December 28th 1916 – Relieved and proceeded to Derry until January 5th 1917. Further light action and enemy trench raiding parties.

February 2nd 1917 – B and D companies went to Kemmel Chateau. C and D companies went to Derry Huts.

March/April 1917 – Retraining and light action.

May 17th 1917 – Left Kemmel Shelterings and joined the Brigade in the St Omer area. The Rangers were then entrained from Bailleul to Arques on the 18th and on to Bavenghen-Les-Geninghen.

May 29th 1917 – The 6th was marched to Arques on the 29th, Staple on the 30th and finally 'Clare Camp' on the 31st.

June 4th 1917 – Members of the Battalion carried out a courageous and successful raid (in strength) on enemy trenches south of Petit Bois.

June 5th, 6th, 7th 1917 – Action before Wytschaete. This was a major action.

June 9th, 1917 – Relieved to Locre (Loker) area.

July 23rd, 1917 – The Connaught Rangers were taken by road and train to Winnezeele and billeted at Briel.

July 30th, 1917 – Proceeded to Brandhoek area and billeted in hutments in a field south of Poperinghe.

July 31st, 1917– The third battle of Ypres (Ieper) started on a large front. The Connaught Rangers were in reserve.

August 1st, 1917 – 5AM. Ordered to the north east of Ypres (Ieper) then by train to Goldfish Chateau. Then marched to Ypres (Ieper) and the Menin Gate and thence to the left sector of the IX Corps front. There followed action around Messines (Mesen), Wyschaete Ridge, The Wulvergham, Wyschaete Road and Diependhal.

August 2nd, 1917 – Battalion HQ was now in the 'Cambridge Trench'. At 8pm the Connaughts moved up the Potijze road, under a very heavy bombardment to the Blue Line, in close support of the 6th Battalion, Royal Irish Regiment. The 6th Rangers relieved them and moved forward to the Black Line. A, B, and C companies were on the reverse slope of Frezenberg Ridge, while D Company was on the forward slope in full view of the enemy.

The 6th battalion was now in reserve to the 47th Brigade which had suffered heavy losses at Frezenberg Ridge. A stretcher-bearing party of 200 men, 50 from each company of the 6th Connaughts, was sent out to bring in the wounded from the old enemy front system.

Major-General Jeudwine of the 55th division wrote to Major-General Hickey of the 16th Division:

We are very much indebted to you for the brave and devoted work of 150 men of the 6th Connaught Rangers who were lent to us as stretcher-bearers. They had about the hardest task that any stretcher-bearers have had in this war – a very long carry under severe fire over ground which was difficult beyond description. From all I hear they performed this task most gallantly – not I am afraid without severe casualties to themselves …

Col Thurston R.A.M.C. also wrote to the commanding Officer of the 6th:

The assistance rendered by men of your battalion to R.A.M.C. in bringing back wounded during the recent fighting is much appreciated. They worked splendidly and showed great self-sacrifice and devotion to duty.

August 3rd, 1917 – Shelling continued throughout August 3rd. It was impossible to do much work on the wrecked lines which were nearly all under water. The Rangers' casualties were heavy, especially among the Lewis gunners of A Company. The men were almost continuously under fire without any opportunity of replying.

August 4th, 1917 – The weather improved on August the 4th and this allowed fourteen enemy spotter aircraft to fly over the lines during the afternoon. During the night shelling continued to be heavy and the battalion had its first experience of mustard gas. The gas shells were sent over with trench-mortar shells.

August 5th 1917 – In the early morning two enemy aircraft flew low over the front lines and were followed by heavy and accurate shelling at noon.

The rain continued incessantly and the mud was so bad in the trenches that neither rifles nor Lewis guns would fire. Despite the atrocious weather conditions the Germans mounted a spirited attack which was driven off in fierce hand-to-hand fighting with bayonets and grenades.

The mud was everywhere knee deep and in some places waist deep. Very heavy shelling continued again between 9pm and 11pm At midnight the 6th battalion Connaught Rangers were relieved in the midst of another outbreak of very heavy shelling.

The original trench line on Frezenberg Ridge can clearly be seen as the darker shadow starting above the letter T and continuing to the former German bunker below B.

March 1918

For the next eight months the 6th Connaughts continued with a series of minor engagements and by 1918 found itself at Villers Faucon. After the celebrations of St Patrick's Day were over the men were sent out on trench raiding parties and brought back a number of German prisoners. Under 'interrogation' the prisoners stated that a very major German attack would take place on the 20th of March. This was correct information but the German High Command postponed the attack at the last moment and when nothing happened on the 20th the British High Command did not then expect an imminent attack.

During the night of March 20th–21st a very dense fog set in over the whole front reducing visibility to 15 yards (12 metres) by morning. At noon the Germans opened their attack with a fierce bombardment followed by a massed assault of Storm Troopers. The 6th Battalion Connaught Rangers was almost annihilated in the subsequent fighting. In the enforced retreat the Rangers held their ground to the end. They were the last to leave the field.

On April 13th the remnants of the 6th Bn reached Drionville where they received orders that they were to be transferred to the 2n Bn Leinster Regiment. A small officer corps was retained to train newly arriving American NCOs but by July no more Americans had arrived and on the 31st July 1918 the 6th Connaught Ranger officer corps was transferred to the 5th Bn Connaught Rangers. The 6th Battalion the Connaught Rangers was no more.

BIBLIOGRAPHY

Guillemont, Somme, Michael Stedman, Leo Cooper, Pen & Sword Books, 1998.
The Fierce Light, Anne Powell, Sutton Publishing Limited 2006.
The German Army at Passchendaele, Jack Sheldon, Pen & Sword Books 2007.

Belfast Enlistees in the
6th Connaught Rangers
1914–1918

The list on the following pages contains names of those men who are, because of their regimental number, believed to have enlisted in the 6th Connaughts in Belfast, mainly in November 1914 to March 1915. It was compiled from the Connaught Rangers regimental medal rolls at the National Archives in Kew and the *Soldiers Died in the Great War* listings.

The column headed 'END OF SERVICE' contains a reference to how the soldier came to leave their role in the ranks. The column to the right, headed 'DATE' indicates the date that came into effect.

The abbreviations which explain the 'end of service' describe the following:

392 iii (c)	Discharged under King's Regulations (1912) Paragraph 392 within three months of enlistment considered unfit for service.
392 iii (cc)	Discharged under King's Regulations (1912) Paragraph 392 with more than three months service but considered unfit for further military service.
392 xvi	Discharged under King's Regulations (1912) Paragraph 392 no longer physically fit for service.
392 xxv	Discharged under King's Regulations (1912) Paragraph 392 his service being no longer required.
Class Z	Transferred to Class Z of the Army Reserve. Men in this Class were demobilised but were obliged to return to the army if recalled. This Reserve was established at the end of 1918 in case Germany did not honour the armistice and a later peace treaty, and was abolished in March 1920.
Commission	Became an officer in the CR (Connaught Rangers) or other regiment.
Deserted	A man who left his unit without permission. It should be noted that those who deserted while away from the front were often treated leniently.
Died	Died (usually of illness or old age) while in the army, but not in a way connected to military action.
KIA	Killed in Action.

Ser. No.	Rank	Name	Award	Place of Birth	Residence	End of Service	Date
2230	Private	McCann, Daniel				Class Z	15/06/1919
2235	Private	McLaughlin, Michael				Class Z	19/06/1919
2241	Sergeant	Goodwin, James		Belfast	Belfast	KIA	16/08/1917
2248	Private	Mallon, Thomas		Belfast	Belfast	KIA	04/03/1916
2256	Private	McKeown, Joseph		Belfast	Belfast	Died	14/05/1917
2259	Private	Kelly, Michael				392 iii (cc)	26/03/1915
2261	Private	McBrinn, Joseph Hugh				Class Z	19/03/1919
2269	Private	O'Connor, Patrick				392 iii (cc)	26/03/1915
2270	Sergeant	McGuigan, John				Discharged and commissioned in CR	30/10/1917
2272	Private	Devlin, Patrick	MM			Class Z	18/02/1919
2276	Private	McKenna, Patrick				Class Z	01/03/1919
2279	Colour Sergeant	Nulty, James				Commission in CR	26/06/1917
2281	Sergeant	Pollock, James Joseph	MM			Class Z	13/05/1919
2293	Sergeant	Kearney, James	MM			Promoted to commission in Inniskillings	29/01/1918
2294	Private	Cawley, William				Deserted	05/03/1917
2314	Private	Logan, John		Carrickfergus, Co Antrim	Belfast	KIA	05/03/1917
2324	Private	McMurrough, William Leo				Unclear	05/03/1916

Ser. No.	Rank	Name	Award	Place of Birth	Residence	End of Service	Date
2328	Private	McKenna, John Henry		Belfast	Belfast	KIA	07/06/1917
2329	Private	Runaghan, John		Belfast	Belfast	KIA	28/03/1916
2332	Private	Conway, John					
2333	Private	Magill, Isaac Patrick					
2334	Private	Donnelly, Michael				Class Z	10/04/1919
2336	Private	Fogarty, Robert James				Class Z	09/05/1919
2337	Private	Drain, John		Belfast	Belfast	KIA	09/09/1916
2339	Private	Prenter, Thomas Patrick				Class Z	24/02/1919
2341	Private	Healy, Michael Patrick		Belfast	Belfast	KIA	04/05/1916
2346	Private	Thompson, George				Discharged on demob	31/03/1920
2350	Private	Downey, Richard				392 xvi	07/02/1918
2352	Private	Hanna, Joseph				Class Z	20/02/1919
2358	Private	Alexander, Samuel		Glasgow	Belfast	KIA	16/08/1917
2361	Private	Hughes, John				Deserted	08/12/1916
2363	Corporal	Reilly, Frank				392 xvi	24/04/1919
2364	Private	Canavan, James		Belfast	Belfast	Died	02/03/1916
2367	Colour Sergeant	Hyland, James Patrick				Promoted to commission	12/01/1916
2368	Private	Lyons, John		Belfast	Belfast	KIA	04/05/1916
2369	Private	O'Toole, Peter				Class Z	20/03/1919

Ser. No.	Rank	Name	Award	Place of Birth	Residence	End of Service	Date
2370	Private	McKinley, Richard				Class Z	04/03/1919
2371	Private	Runaghan, Alexander				392 xvi	17/06/1918
2372	Private	Dempsey, Patrick Joseph				Class Z	15/02/1919
2381	Private	Smyth, William John				Deserted	14/09/1918
2384	Sergeant	Tully, James				392 iii (cc)	26/03/1915
2386	Private	McKinney, Felix		Belfast	Belfast	KIA	05/03/1916
2387	Private	Goodall, John				392 iii (cc)	12/05/1915
2392	Private	Hillman, John				Class Z	19/03/1919
2394	Private	McKillen, Patrick		Belfast	Belfast	Died	07/08/1917
2395	Sergeant	Cush, John				Class Z	29/02/1919
2402	Private	Bloomer, Andrew		Belfast	Belfast	Died	21/03/1918
2408	Private	McGinney, Patrick		Belfast	Belfast	KIA	03/09/1916
2411	Private	Burns, John		Belfast	Belfast	KIA	25/03/1916
2417	Private	Shannon, William John				392 xvi	28/08/1918
2420	Private	Neeson, Patrick				Class Z	08/03/1919
2423	Private	McGrath, William				392 xvi	16/05/1919
2425	Private	Harte, Thomas				Deserted	01/11/1916
2426	Private	Smith, Terence				Deserted	17/12/1916
2428	Private	O'Neill, Thomas				Deserted	22/04/1916

Ser. No.	Rank	Name	Award	Place of Birth	Residence	End of Service	Date
2429	Sergeant	Millar, William				Commission in 3 CR	30/07/1918
2430	Private	Maynes, Henry				Class Z	19/03/1919
2431	Private	Toner, Michael Joseph	MM				
2432	Private	McErlane, John J				Class Z	15/03/1919
2436	Private	Prenter, James				392 xvi	24/04/1917
2437	Private	McKernon, John		Crumlin, Co. Antrim	Whitewell, Co. Antrim	Died	9/04/1916
2442	Private	Lavery, John		Warren Point, Co. Down	Belfast	KIA	27/01/1916
2445	Private	Oprey, Peter Joseph MM				Deserted	23/02/1918
2453	Private	Parkinson, Joseph				Class Z	25/02/1919
2457	Private	Kennedy, Michael		Ballynahill, Queen's County		KIA	08/04/1916
2458	Private	Henry, Daniel				Class Z	23/02/1920
2459	Lance Corporal	Hughes, John James				392 xvi	14/03/1918
2462	Private	Kavanagh, George				392 xxv	07/01/1919
2463	Corporal	Liddy, Joseph				Deserted	12/12/1917
2464	Sergeant	Conway, James				392 xvi	06/06/1916
2465	Private	Cassidy, John				392 xvi	24/05/1918
2466	Private	Magee, Hugh					

Ser. No.	Rank	Name	Award	Place of Birth	Residence	End of Service	Date
2470	Private	McAuley, John				Class Z	17/04/1919
2474	Private	O'Hare, Edward				392 xvi	28/12/1916
2475	Sergeant	Shannon, John Patrick				Class Z	14/06/1919
2476	Private	Moore, Thomas Francis				Class Z	15/03/1919
2477	Corporal	Seary, Brian					
2481	Private	Sherrie, James				Deserted	02/10/1917
2483	Acting Sergeant	Lawson, Joseph				392 xxv	09/01/1919
2486	Sergeant	Hackett, Augustine		Dublin	Belfast	KIA	19/02/1917
2487	WO Cl 2	McKeown, John	MM			Class Z	19/03/1919
2488	Private	Hunt, Edward		London	London	KIA	08/01/1917
2490	Private	Shannon, Patrick		Belfast	Belfast	Died	06/06/1916
2492	Private	Doherty, Joseph				Class Z	20/03/1919
2494	Private	Davey, Maurice Joseph				392 xvi	15/04/1918
2495	Private	Maginness, James				Class Z	27/03/1919
2496	Lance Corporal	Brennan, Robert				392 xvi	08/05/1916
2497	Corporal	Brennan, Michael				Class Z	09/05/1919
2499	Private	Larmour, Thomas				392 xvi	19/02/1918

Ser. No.	Rank	Name	Award	Place of Birth	Residence	End of Service	Date
2500	Private	Blake, John Patrick				Class Z	20/02/1919
2502	Private	McIlvenny, Robert		Belfast	Belfast	Died	09/10/1918
2506	Private	Meenan, Bernard					14/06/1918
2507	Private	Kinney, Charles				Class Z	09/05/1919
2512	Private	Duff, Daniel		Belfast	Belfast	KIA	14/10/1918
2513	Private	Nugent, Michael John				Class Z	23/02/1919
2516	Private	Napier, James				Class Z	08/05/1919
2518	Private	Murphy, Alexander				392 xvi	04/01/1916
2521	Private	O'Neill, Thomas				Class Z	20/02/1919
2522	Sergeant	Crowley, Patrick				Class Z	03/03/1919
2525	Private	Campbell, Patrick				392 xvi	10/06/1918
2529	Private	Walsh, Joseph				Class Z	15/03/1919
2529	Private	Sweeney, Michael				392 xvi	11/01/1919
2530	Private	McGreevy, Hugh				Class Z	09/05/1919
2536	Private	Digney, Charles					
2539	Private	Ferron, James				Deserted	24/10/1917
2542	Private	Campton, James				392 iii(c)	08/01/1915
2547	Private	Magee, James				392 iii(c)	09/02/1915
2549	Private	Straney, Hugh				Class Z	20/03/1919

Ser. No.	Rank	Name	Award	Place of Birth	Residence	End of Service	Date
2552	Private	McGuckian, Henry				Class Z	31/03/1919
2558	Private	Malone, Joseph				392 xvi	20/12/1917
2564	Private	English, Thomas		Belfast		KIA	03/08/1917
2569	Private	Skillen, John					
2572	Corporal	Connolly, Thomas James				392 xvi	05/08/1916
2574	Private	Connolly, James				392 xvi	12/06/1917
2576	Private	McIlroy, Patrick				KIA	12/01/1917
2579	Private	Kane, John		Belfast		392 xvi	09/06/1916
2580	Private	Small, John				392 xvi	15/05/1918
2583	Sergeant	Conlon, James				Deserted	01/10/1917
2585	Sergeant	McNally, James				Died	22/09/1916
2591	Corporal	McCann, James		Belfast		392 xvi	11/06/1917
2592	Corporal	Turley, James				392 xvi	28/05/1917
2593	Private	O'Hare, Owen				392 xvi	28/08/1918
2594	Sergeant	Leetle, Michael	MM			392 xvi	18/01/1917
2595	Private	McDermott, Patrick				Class Z	02/03/1919
2605	Private	Hockney, Albert					

In addition to those included in the list above, Belfast residence has been established for the following who, at some point, served with the 6th Connaughts:

Ser. No.	Rank	Name	Award	Place of Birth	Residence	End of Service	Date
1514	Pte	Joseph Burns				Died of wounds	080/9/1916
2195	Sgt	Daniel McKenna				KIA	26/07/1916
2197	Pte	John Sweeney				Died	31/01/1916
2376	Pte	William Stewart					
2759	Pte	John Rush				KIA	05/05/1916
2802	Pte	Michael Ferguson					
2835	Pte	William Reid				Died	18/11/1918
2845	Pte	James O'Reilly					
2868	Pte	Edward Hughes				KIA	17/05/1916
3490	Pte	Daniel McGlade				KIA	31/07/1916
3566	Pte	Hugh Joseph Barr				KIA	03/02/1916
3578	Pte	John Rice					
3579	Pte	Alexander Steensen				KIA	30/05/1916
3620	Pte	Patrick McCormack				KIA	07/02/1916
3643	Pte	Henry Shaw					
3923	Pte	James Conway				KIA	03/09/1916
3942	Pte	Patrick Gawley				KIA	04/06/1917

Ser. No.	Rank	Name	Award	Place of Birth	Residence	End of Service	Date
3977	Pte	John Short				Died	23/11/1917
4030	Pte	John Smith					
4057	Pte	John Breen				Died	10/10/1918
4189	Pte	Patrick Robb					
4283	Cpl	Henry 'Harry' Patrick Walsh					
4308	Pte	Francis McCrossan				KIA	10/03/1916
4332	Pte	Joseph Crowley				KIA	03/09/1916
4346	Pte	Edward Casey				Died	26/12/1917
4347	Pte	David Corbett				KIA	04/03.1916
4373	Pte	William John McCartan				KIA	28/01/1916
4385	Pte	James Carragher				Regarded as dead	09/09/1916
4414	Pte	William Ferris				KIA	03/09/1916
4418	Pte	Joseph McKay				KIA	20/11/1917
4441	Pte	John O'Neill					
4567	Pte	Peter O'Donnell					
4583	Pte	Joseph Mayne				Died	10/01/1918
4587	Pte	Thomas Mullan				Died of wounds	17/09/1918
4605	Pte	William Hutton				KIA	08/03/1917
4609	Pte	Charles McNally				Died	18/07/1916

Ser. No.	Rank	Name	Award	Place of Birth	Residence	End of Service	Date
4640	Pte	James Crawford				KIA	05/03/1916
4669	Pte	James Brown				KIA	03/09/1916
4682	Pte	Robert Herbert Boggs				KIA	27/04/1918
4694	Pte	Thomas Wylie				Died of wounds	04/09/1918
4697	Pte	Alfred Broderick				KIA	03/09/1916
4698	Pte	William Toner				KIA	08/10/1918
4746	Pte	Frank McCarton				Regarded as dead	03/09/1916
6449	Pte	John Mellon				KIA	20/11/1917
6489	Pte	Francis McCoy				KIA	20/11/1917
6686	Pte	Thomas O'Hagan					
7481	Pte	James McIlwee				KIA	03/08/1917
7986	Sgt	Patrick O'Hare					
9416	Acting Sgt	Hugh Haslam				Died	25/08/1917
10919	Pte	Hugh Malone				Died	23/03/1918
18173	Pte	Alexander McCloskey				Died	21/03/1918

How to find out more about the 6th Connaught Rangers

Richard S. Grayson

PUBLICATIONS

There are several books which tell the story of the 6th Connaught Rangers in different ways. The most detailed is the official history: H.F.N. Jourdain and Edward Fraser, *The Connaught Rangers: Vol. III*, (1928). This is out of print and can only be found in a few libraries, although it is very largely based on the battalion war diaries (see 'National Archives' below) which can be seen easily. Another out of print book, but more widely available in libraries and second-hand, is Terence Denman, *Ireland's Unknown Soldiers: The 16th (Irish) Division in the Great War* (1992). There are over 10,000 words on the battalion (twice the amount of material in my section in this booklet) in my book, *Belfast Boys: How Unionists and Nationalists Fought and Died Together in the First World War* (2009).

A new edition of Rowland Feilding's letters is *War Letters to a Wife: France and Flanders, 1915–1919* (1929, 2001 edn.). The memoirs of another officer with the 6th Connaughts, Charles Brett, were published by the Somme Association in 2007: *Charles Brett MC: an Irish soldier with the Connaught Rangers in World War I*.

An interesting chapter is: John Morrissey, 'A Lost Heritage: The Connaught Rangers and Multivocal Irishness', in Mark McCarthy, ed., *Ireland's Heritage: Critical perspectives on Memory and Identity* (2005), pp. 71–87.

The battalion is covered in passing in Tom Johnstone, *Orange, Green and Khaki: The Story of the Irish Regiments in the Great War, 1914–18*, (Dublin, 1992), and Steven Moore, *The Irish on the Somme: A Battlefield Guide to the Irish Regiments in the Great War and the Monuments in their Memory* (2005).

The most detailed guide to the cemeteries on the Western Front has for many years been *Before Endeavours Fade: Guide to the Battlefields of the First World War* by Rose E.B. Coombs. First published in 1976, it is regularly updated. A more specific guide of relevance to the 6th Connaughts is Michael Stedman, *Battleground Europe: Guillemont* (1998).

ONLINE RECORDS

www.ancestry.co.uk has records from the National Archives in Kew of soldiers who were awarded (or applied for) a pension between 1914 and 1920, plus the service records which survived the London Blitz in 1940 (around 25 per cent of records). Individuals can be searched for, but there is a charge for viewing the original records. The site also contains all medal rolls from 1914–18 (see also 'National Archives' below), so it is likely that all soldiers will be somewhere on this site.

www.cwgc.org.uk contains the records of the Commonwealth War Graves Commission, and is the best place to start for a dead soldier.

Listings of all dead servicemen can be found in *Soldiers Died in the Great War* and *Officers Died in the Great War* which are published by the Naval and Military Press on CD-Rom (see below) but are also available at:

> http://search.ancestry.co.uk/search/db.aspx?dbid=1543

These records are searchable in a number of ways, including regiment/battalion, place of birth, residence and enlistment.

Ireland's Memorial Records are now available on CD (see below) but are also searchable online at: for a charge at http://search.ancestry.co.uk/search/db.aspx?dbid=1633. It is widely regarded as a problematic source as it claims to contain the names of 49,000 'Irishmen' who died in the war. However, estimates of the 'Irish dead' now go as low as 25,000, with most academics agreed on around 35,000. The problem with this listing of 49,000 is that it includes all those who died in Irish regiments (many of whom would have been transferred from English, Scottish or Welsh regiments), and does not include the many Irishmen who died in non-Irish units. However, it is still a valuable source.

CD-ROMs

Soldiers Died in the Great War and *Officers Died in the Great War* are published by the Naval and Military Press on CD-Rom (www.naval-military-press.com) This source is also available online (see above).

Ireland's Memorial Records are now available on CD at:
www.eneclann.ie/acatalog/ENEC011.html and are also searchable online (see above). The soldiers' wills kept in the National Archives in Dublin have been produced on CD-Rom by Eneclann, based in Dublin (www.eneclann.ie)

NATIONAL ARCHIVES

The main resources documenting the day-to-day activities of the 6th Connaught Rangers are the battalion, brigade and divisional war diaries at the National Archives in Kew. The key files are:

> WO 95/1970: 6th Connaught Rangers
> WO 95/1969: 47 Brigade
> WO 95/1955: 16th Division, December 1915 to April 1917
> WO 95/1956: 16th Division, May 1917 to April 1918
> WO 158/416: 16th Division Operations, 7–9 June 1917

It is not necessary to visit Kew to see all of these, as both WO 95/1970 and WP 95/1969 are available (for a charge) on line at:

> www.nationalarchives.gov.uk/documentsonline/war-diaries.asp

Meanwhile, the medal roll of all individuals who received service and/or gallantry medals can be viewed and (for a charge) downloaded at:

> www.nationalarchives.gov.uk/documentsonline/medals.asp

These rolls can also be viewed via www.ancestry.co.uk (see 'Online Records' above).

Other medal rolls, only in hard copy at Kew, are the regimental lists, in which individuals are listed largely alphabetically. Officers are listed in WO 329/2255, with other ranks on:

> WO 329/1688   WO 329/1689   WO 329/1690
> WO 329/1691

Many individuals in the battalion also appear on the medal rolls of the Leinster Regiment:

> WO 329/1699   WO 329/1700   WO 329/1701
> WO 329/1702
> WO 329/2815

Individual records for officers are held mainly in the WO 339 category (but also some in WO 374) at Kew. None of these are available online, but unlike service records for non-officers, all records have, in theory, survived.

If you do not have access to the internet, you can write for guidance to:
> The National Archives, Kew, Richmond, Surrey, TW9 4DU

NEWSPAPERS

Newspapers are hard to use without exact dates, but all Belfast newspapers are available in the Belfast Newspaper Library, the British Newspaper Library in Colindale, and the National Library in Dublin. The Belfast Newspaper Library allows both photocopying and the taking of photographs with a digital camera for personal use. The main Belfast newspapers from the period are:

Belfast Evening Telegraph (which dropped *Evening* from its title in April 1918)
Belfast News Letter
Irish News
Northern Whig

Belfast's newspapers are an unusually rich source. Unlike many other local papers, they carried much information on soldiers of all ranks, with the *Belfast Evening Telegraph* often including photos of the killed and wounded. In addition to formal reports and listings, 'In Memoriam' notices placed by families, especially in the *Telegraph* and *Irish News*, are extremely useful. In searching for information on an individual, bear in mind that details often did not appear for some months after what we now know to be a date of death.

Poscard sent home by a 6th Connaught Ranger from the training camp in Aldershot, 1915. Set up on Gun Hill in the 1860s, the Aldershot gun fires at 9.30pm to call the troops back to barracks, in addition to the traditional 1 o'clock firing

Useful Addresses

BELFAST CENTRAL LIBRARY
Royal Avenue
Belfast, BT1 1EA
Telephone: (028) 9050 9150
E-mail: info@libraries.belfast-elb.gov.uk
Website: www.belb.org.uk

BELFAST CENTRAL LIBRARY –
NEWSPAPER LIBRARY
Library St
Belfast, BT1 1EA
Telephone: 028 9050 9117

GENERAL REGISTER OFFICE
Northern Ireland Statistics and Research Agency
Oxford House, 49/55 Chichester Street
Belfast, BT1 4HL
Telephone: (028) 9025 2000
E-mail: gro.nisra@dfpni.gov.uk (Birth, Death
and Marriage Certificate Enquiries)
Website: www.groni.gov.uk

BELFAST REGISTRAR'S OFFICE
Belfast City Council
City Hall, Belfast, BT1 5GS
Telephone: (028) 90270274
E-mail: registrar@belfastcity.gov.uk

CONNAUGHT RANGERS ASSOCIATION
King House
Boyle, Co. Roscommon
Ireland
E-mail: info@connaughtrangersassoc.com
Website: www.connaughtrangersassoc.com

IRISH DEFENCES FORCES MILITARY
ARCHIVES
Cathal Brugha Barracks
Rathmines, Dublin 6
Telephone: (01) 804 6457
Website: www.military.ie/dfhq/archives/arch.htm

LINEN HALL LIBRARY
17 Donegall Square North
Belfast, BT1 5GD
Telephone: (028) 9032 1707
E-mail: info@linenhall.com
Website: www.linenhall.com/Home/home.html

NATIONAL ARCHIVES OF IRELAND
Bishop Street
Dublin 8
Telephone: (01) 407 2300
E-mail: mail@nationalarchives.ie
Website: www.nationalarchives.ie

NATIONAL LIBRARY OF IRELAND
Kildare Street
Dublin 2
Telephone: (01) 603 0200
E-mail: info@nli.ie
Website: www.nli.ie

PUBLIC RECORD OFFICE OF
NORTHERN IRELAND
2 Titanic Boulevard
Titanic Quarter
Belfast, BT3 9HQ
Telephone: (028) 9053 4800
Website: www.proni.gov.uk

THE NATIONAL ARCHIVES
Kew
Richmond
Surrey, TW9 4DU
Website: www.nationalarchives.gov.uk

ULSTER HISTORICAL FOUNDATION
49 Malone Road
Belfast, BT9 6RY
Telephone: (028) 9066 1988
E-mail: enquiry@uhf.org.uk
Website: www.ancestryireland.com